MW00617941

The Daughters of Heaven

Living in the Presence of the Divine Mother

Michael Mirdad

GRAIL
PRESS

The Daughters of Heaven
Living in the Presence of the Divine Mother

GRAIL
PRESS

PO Box 1908
Sedona, AZ 86339
(360) 671-8349

office@MichaelMirdad.com
www.MichaelMirdad.com

Book cover and interior design by
Robert Lanphear
www.lanpheardesign.com

The Daughters of Heaven/
Michael Mirdad

ISBN: 978-0-9600597-2-0

ACKNOWLEDGMENTS

For the creation of this book, I thank God (the Father, Mother, and the Christ), as that is the Source of this material. I also thank my students who helped to co-create the sacred space for this book and activation to come through. Thank you to all those who helped to proofread and edit. A very special thanks goes out to my (personal and professional) "team members." Bless you and thank you Lonnie & Connie Frisbee for being such Lights in the world—even through times of religious persecution. Lastly, I want to thank all of the Daughters of Heaven, who live all around the world, whose (conscious or unconscious) prayers reached Heaven and activated this announcement of their coming to the world.

The Consciousness (Kingdom)
of God (Heaven) is within you.

–Jesus

Note from the author:

The Bible quotes used within this book are my own interpretations. Although in most cases they are nearly the same as the standard interpretations, these will feel more mystical and loving. This captures more of the original meaning and allows the quote to take on a new life.

Table of Contents

Announcing the Final Wave of Lightworkers

One day, when I was speaking/teaching at our spiritual center—The Global Center for Christ Consciousness—in Sedona, Arizona, **an announcement came out of my mouth for all Lightworkers and for all people on the spiritual path.**

Our usual procedure for our Sacred Sunday Services is for me to ask the audience what topics they would like me to cover during the talk. Then I launch into a spontaneous talk channeled by Spirit that weaves most, or all, of the requested topics together—and more. These talks are typically well received for their depth and practicality. On this *particular* day, however, after I began sharing on the topics that attendees called out for—which included ascended masters and healing of the soul—I was being guided to cap things off by introducing a topic that is *new* to humanity—at least new on a *conscious* level.

The topic was about **a new and profound group of individuals that are emerging to put the finishing touches on God's Plan for the awakening of humanity. This group is known as the "Daughters of Heaven."** The Daughters of Heaven are incarnating as extensions of the Divine Mother and are acting as spiritual midwives to assist in the birthing of a new world. Their part in the Divine Plan is more about holding a *deep*, spiritual presence, than it is about doing *external* work—although they very often will choose to do a blend of both.

As soon as I mentioned the title of the topic, there was a palpable shift, or activation, in the room (as well as for most of the viewers who were attending online). The topic led many to experience very deep emotions: tears, feeling "seen," a shift into various dimensions, and/or a major "activation" in their soul.

The first time I was made aware of the Daughters of Heaven goes back many years when I heard the name in my mind during a workshop. Years later, in a different workshop, I had the attendees do a particular exercise that ended up igniting a blissful vision in my mind of something that looked like goddesses bringing the Light and Love of God to the world. Several years later, I received further information about the Daughters of Heaven, but I never spoke about it until now.

At the start of this *particular* Sacred Service, as I was looking around the room to hear the various topics being requested, my eyes kept shifting back to the front-center of the room (without being too obvious) because **I saw the image of a faint, transparent-like angel.** This angel was apparently there to give me permission to introduce this new topic—the "Daughters of Heaven"—but this was not completely clear to me until I was part-way through the talk. It was at that point that **I closed my eyes for a moment to receive *internal* confirmation for the *external* guidance I was receiving from the angel.** Once this confirmation was received, I began sharing on this topic—even though I kept mentally juggling the question of exactly how *much* I should share. I then added more details about this topic in our services over the next few weeks.

Almost immediately after that Sunday talk, I experienced some dreams and visions that confirmed that **there is indeed an incredible new wave of Beings of Light that are descending from the heavens**—as part of a "great cosmic speed-up" designed to bring humanity into the "homestretch" (as it were) of our life on Earth. This group of powerful beings is moving closer to the material universe—in order to assist in our return Home. These beings include a new wave of angels (previously unknown to mankind), as well as these wonderful human beings we are now calling, "the Daughters of Heaven."

Days later, I was awakened in the middle of the night with a "download" of enough material to write a book on this topic—the book you now hold in your hands. By morning I told a few friends that I had just written a book overnight called, "The Daughters of Heaven." They seemed excited, but not totally surprised. It was clear, however, that **this material is not just a book or a lecture; it is more like a time-released "activation"—and the time for its release is now!**

The information that came through during these talks, and in this book, are the result of having a close relationship, throughout most of my life, with

the Holy Spirit (Divine Mother). I'm certain that my workshops over the past 30-40 years—on Mastery and Christ Consciousness—as well as my practice of daily communion with God and my current, monthly day of devotional prayer (attended by my students from around the world) have also played a part. After all, **it's quite natural to reap good fruit from a tree well planted and nurtured into maturity.**

CHAPTER ONE

The Call to Assist in the Grand Awakening

THERE IS A PLAN

It would be impossible to discuss the Daughters of Heaven—or any other faction of Lightworkers—without first explaining that **God has a plan for the awakening of mankind**. This plan has two primary phases: 1) To awaken mankind 2) To awaken all other beings in the universe. This plan is guaranteed to succeed. The part we play only affects *when* and how *smoothly* this process will occur.

⟿⟾

God chose us before the foundation of the world, to be holy and blameless . . . God loved us and chose us in Christ to be holy and without fault in His eyes.

–Ephesians 1:4

OUR ORIGIN & DESTINY:
FROM LEMURIA TO TODAY

The Daughters of Heaven, like all Children of God, began as beings of Pure Light (being made in God's Pure Image) and to this Pure Light, we are now being called to return. But these beings eventually splintered off into astral and etheric realms. Eventually, those who were choosing to enter physical density gathered in Lemuria—the lost continent in the Pacific Ocean and the original Garden of Eden. This civilization was predominantly a matriarchal society—led by Lightworkers, and a portion of the Daughters of Heaven. These groups of souls dedicated to our return Home were collectively called, "The Children of the Sun." The people who once populated Lemuria were guided by etheric-like goddesses, who were in contact with Lightbeings known as the Arcturians.

After the demise of Lemuria, Atlantis became the dominant civilization—from 200,000 BC until 10,000 BC. Here, the Lightworkers were known as the "Children of the Law of One." This group included historic characters such as Akhenaton, Ra Ta, Isis, and Hermes (also known as Thoth), to name but a few. **The primary directive of *this* group**

was to anchor the Light of God into the Earth's grids and into the consciousness of Earth's inhabitants.

Much later—around 1,000 BC—the Daughters of Heaven came to Earth as some of the Israelites (Is-Real-Lights), and a few hundred years later as the Essenes, who eventually authored the Dead Sea Scrolls and *personally* taught such great souls as Mother Mary, John the Baptist, and Jesus himself. These dear souls (the Daughters of Heaven) also came to Earth as the women who surrounded and supported Jesus, Mother Mary, and eventually Mary Magdalene.

During the time of Jesus, the primary role models for the Daughters of Heaven (as we know them today) were Mother Mary, Mary Magdalene, and a woman named Thecla (all of which will be discussed later in this material).

Once the blueprint had been set, the coming Daughters of Heaven would *often* incarnate at varying times, as they trained for their eventual return as one collective for the Grand Awakening. During some of those previous incarnations, they lived as priests, nuns, mystics, poets, artists, and many other roles. But they were always feeling called to God. It is only NOW that those who had originally splintered off, and those who incarnated, are coming together in one lifetime. **They are now incarnating in the same, current generation because it is time for a global ascension.**

Returning now as a full collective, they began to incarnate roughly seventy years ago in order to assist with our ascension process, but most were not consciously aware (other than hints) of who they were nor what they were here to do. It was not yet the right time for this to be in their conscious awareness, and therefore, it had to wait until after 2020 (20/20)—a year that symbolized "clear seeing." But now, **their activation has begun! The Divine Mother has struck the bell that is reverberating in the hearts and souls of these blessed beings.** And they will now begin to rise, shake off the dust of amnesia that has accumulated over many millennia, find each other through networking, and celebrate their activation into service. Then, **their love, devotion, and communion with God will reach new heights, as has never been seen before.**

For now we see only a reflection of the good that is to come, but eventually we will embody it and experience it directly. Now I know things only in part; then I shall know all things fully, even as I am fully known.

–1 Corinthians 13:12

The timing is just right for the Daughters of Heaven to awaken. Prophecies from every culture and continent tell us that **NOW is the time for a major global shift—in life and in consciousness.** This means that, although things are becoming their darkest on this planet, the Light of God is just around the corner. This becomes obvious when we see the condition of the world and its politics, as well as seeing that for the first time in history, the number of people and Nations who do *NOT* believe in God is at its all-time high. And yet, we are simultaneously seeing a resurgence of interest in Jesus and the "Jesus Revolution" movement—via movies and cable shows, as well as in music. **The Light is growing, as is the darkness, but only *one* is real.** These two polarities will now grow several times greater, forcing mankind to make a choice as to which one will be their "truth."

It is the destiny of all souls to develop a closer "walk with God" and a closer relationship with Christ and the Holy Spirit (our Divine Mother). As we do, we begin to *embody* what was once mere *glimpses* of Her Presence in our lives. Then, our lives become a reflection of *Her* Consciousness and are filled with experiences of *Her* Love and Abundance— positively affecting our lives and the lives of others around us. This is not *only* a sign of our ascension, but, since it is embodied here and now within us, we might even call it our IN-SCENSION.

CHAPTER TWO

Lightworkers & the Daughters of Heaven

THE SIMILARITIES & DIFFERENCES

In the 1980's, I personally coined the term "Lightworker" as a means of describing any and all beings who *work* (or make an effort) to anchor the *Light* of God into the world/universe. Somehow the term caught on but eventually took on various shallow and/or incorrect interpretations that did not fit the original meaning it was given, which is: **those who *work* at anchoring God's *Light* into the world are *Light-Workers*.**

You are the light of the world ... let your light shine before others, that they may see your good deeds and glorify God in Heaven.

–Jesus

Lightworkers sometimes take the form of healers, spiritual teachers, intuitives, channels, authors, public speakers, life-coaches, yoga instructors, and so on. But they are also moms, dads, schoolteachers, musicians, and just about any other title or role we can imagine. But no matter what we do on this planet, **if we are trying to make this world a better place, a place with more of God's Love and Presence, then we are Lightworkers.**

Lightworkers throughout the universe know that they have a crucial role in this global and universal awakening. They are consciously or unconsciously working with other human beings, elementals, Ascended Masters, etheric beings, animals, Lightbeings, and many others through channeling art, light-language, music, new teachings, and so forth . . . in order to bring balance and higher vibrations to the planet *and* to prepare its inhabitants for a global ascension. It's not unlike a hospital medical team working to raise a person's immunity before they can do surgery.

The "Daughters of Heaven," however, are interested less in actions and information and, instead, focus more on experiencing a sacred relationship with God, as well as basking in the feelings of peace and grace that come from *being* in that Holy Relationship.

Lightworkers enjoy learning and teaching *general* topics of "truth" and broad topics of spirituality, metaphysics, self-help programs, philosophy, and so on. The Daughters of Heaven, however, prefer the *specific* "Truth of God." They enjoy studies on channeling the Consciousness of God, the Christ, and the Divine Mother (Holy Spirit) into the Earthplane, which assures us of not only experiencing a *shift* into higher dimensionality, but also assures us of attaining the *highest* ascension/shift possible.

<hr />

Behold! I tell you a mystery. We shall
no longer see death, but we shall all be
transformed, in a single moment, in the
twinkling of an eye, when time comes to an
end. For the trumpet will sound, and the
dead will be raised imperishable, and we
shall rise to a new dimension.

–1 Corinthians 15:51-52

Lightworkers can appear as individuals or as groups—small or large—sometimes without even consciously knowing it. There are several *small* groups, such as: meditation groups, yoga groups, support groups, 12-Step groups, and so forth. There are also several *large* groups most of us have heard of, or have been a part of, such as: New Thought Churches, the Edgar Cayce Foundation, the Theosophical Society, the Rosicrucians, the Self-Realization Fellowship, the I AM movement, *A Course in Miracles*, the Universal Lightworkers, and so forth, as well as Jewish, Christian, Hindu, Buddhist or Muslim mystics. But **there are also individuals who belong to *no* "group" at all that might *still* be considered Lightworkers.**

The Daughters of Heaven might spend years of their life settling for similar types of religious or spiritual studies, but such things will *not* bring them complete peace—even when studying the most popular topics or the material of the most popular spiritual authors. Like all "students on the path," they may knock on many doors in search of *something*—not always knowing what it is—but **when the doorway to Heaven opens, they know that this, and *only* this, is the fulfillment they were looking for, and is now all they will *ever* accept.**

The path of a Lightworker is wonderful. In fact, it's an absolute necessity for the good of mankind. But while *Lightworkers* are working with Light Beings, Ascended Masters, and fellow Lightworkers to raise the vibrations of the planet and its inhabitants; **the Daughters of Heaven are working with Jesus, Mother Mary, and the Holy Spirit.** It's not so much through *actions*, but—similar to the highest orders of angels—their work is through prayer, holding space, and sharing the palpable effects of their humble and consistent communion with God.

Because of this faithfulness and devotion to God, the Daughters of Heaven carry a natural state of grace. Their approach and relationship to God, however, has never been about "blind superstition." Instead, they have always maintained a *personal* relationship with God, as though God, in whatever form, is right there at their side. That's why they— more than the average person on the path—can more easily talk to God, praise God, dance with God, and feel God's Presence.

Lightworkers are always working to make a difference—whether consciously or unconsciously. As part of their training, they attend spiritual conferences, self-help groups, spiritual workshops, book studies, and/or sound healings. They are often improving their diet, doing yoga, practicing meditation, or spending time doing soul-searching.

The Daughters of Heaven, on the other hand, might very well join *some* of the same groups or experience *some* of the same personal practices as Lightworkers, but with a few distinct differences. **The Daughters of Heaven tend to find themselves yearning for only the highest, deepest, and the most holy teachings.** They don't study for the sake of studying or merely for a mild dose of self-help medicine. They are certainly okay with learning self-improvement, the law of attraction, personal motivation, gaining greater prosperity, or even a healthier lifestyle. **But what *really* feeds them is to hear about God, Jesus, or the Divine Mother.** That's when their ears perk up. That's what feeds their soul and brings them the greatest peace, joy, and comfort.

---

*Beloved Creator, You make known
to me the correct path of life; You
fill me with joy and eternal pleasures
when I enter Your Presence.*

–Psalm 16:11

Lightworkers *can* work alone, but they are usually at their *best* when they work in a group with other Lightworkers. The Daughters of Heaven, on the other hand, are perfectly fine working alone.

They *can* work in groups, but *only* if the members of those groups are committed to prayerfully connecting with God, Jesus, and the Divine Mother (Holy Spirit). If the group lacks this level of depth and commitment, the Daughters of Heaven will likely find themselves participating for a while but feeling out of place—a feeling that is not too uncommon for them.

Lightworkers tend to *serve* the various beings in the Hierarchy of Light—angels, ascended masters, and so forth. But that same hierarchy tends to *serve* the Daughters of Heaven—because of their humility and their closeness to God.

Lightworkers often struggle with the gross contrast between the harsh and abusive Earth dimension versus a universe of Light that they are working so hard to create. The Daughters of Heaven, on the other hand, tend not to get caught up in such disturbing contrasts or the world's apparent battles between Light and dark forces. Instead, **they rely on their faith and their inner knowing that God's Light will prevail,** and therefore it's not really worth it for them to get caught-up in the chaos when they know very well about the inevitable outcome—Heaven on Earth.

Nothing real can be threatened.
Nothing unreal exists. Herein lies
the peace of God.

–A Course in Miracles

Lightworkers are a much larger group of beings than the Daughters of Heaven—hundreds or thousands of times larger. And there is far more diversity of interests and means of service for Lightworkers. They might be Buddhists, Muslims, agnostics, or Pagans. The Daughters of Heaven, on the other hand, have spent less time on the diverse journey and have remained far more faithful and *consistent* on their path—even if they didn't know it at the time. Their interests may have varied a little, but **they've always remained faithful and connected to God, the Divine Mother, Mother Mary, Jesus, and the Christ.**

Lightworkers can include angels, Lightbeings, and humans. The Daughters of Heaven, on the other hand, are almost always human beings. Lightworkers are serving to connect beings throughout the various dimensions of the cosmos. The Daughters of Heaven are connecting God directly to the human race, and are the last group being activated to fulfill this role in the grand awakening.

Again, on one hand **we could say that the Daughters of Heaven are *one* facet of the Universal Lightworkers,** but there is a particular distinction that makes them each unique: Lightworkers are often males, and the type of work they do—teaching, healing, channeling, lecturing, authoring, and so forth—often takes on a masculine vibe. The Daughters of Heaven are much more distinctly feminine. They live with far less *doing* and far more *being*. Lightworkers tend to answer the call to encourage a greater evolution of both human beings *and* the Earth. The Daughters of Heaven, on the other hand, tend to draw the Light of God down *to* the Earth, and enhance our closeness with Spirit. **The Universal Lightworkers are in service to mankind; the Daughters of Heaven are in service to God.**

If it sounds like a comparison is being made between Lightworkers and the Daughters of Heaven, it's because the Daughters of Heaven *are* Lightworkers. But they are a specific faction, or facet, of the Universal Lightworkers. They are a facet that is less focused on their Light-work and more focused on their devotion to God and their love for Jesus and/or the Divine Mother. Another way of saying it is that **Lightworkers are an essential part of God's Plan to bring humanity back *to* Heaven. The Daughters of Heaven are learning to be a living example of what it is like to be *in* Heaven—surrounded by the Love of God—*even* while we are still on Earth.**

CHAPTER THREE

Who Are the Daughters of Heaven?

ALL ABOUT THE DAUGHTERS OF HEAVEN

In one sense, anyone can presently choose to be a Daughter of Heaven simply by hearing and answering the call. In another sense, **the decision to be a Daughter of Heaven was made by some souls many centuries ago, which led them to make decisions related to spiritual devotion and integrity from lifetime to lifetime.**

The Daughters of Heaven are one type of expression of the "divine feminine." They are Children of God who come to observe, feel, and make holy, the world around them. **They tap into the energies of the unseen, and by choosing to "see" at such a high level, they actually ignite what they** observe. They activate a spark where there was once only darkness.

The Daughters of Heaven are embodiments of the Divine Mother—because they *choose* to be and they *live* to be. They are like brides to the Christ—which is the same as saying that "they are souls that are surrendering to Spirit." It's all they can imagine, and nothing else matters.

—⚬—

Seek God above all else, and live
righteously, and He will give you
everything you need.

–Jesus

The Daughters of Heaven might be found dabbling in various forms of philosophy, religion, or self-help practices; but more often than not, **they consciously or unconsciously feel an affinity to God, Jesus the Christ, the Holy Spirit (also known as the Divine Mother Aspect of God), and/or to Mother Mary—even if they don't know why.**

The Daughters of Heaven often feel a call to the awakening of Christ Consciousness throughout the planet—and beyond. But they somehow know that reaching Christ Consciousness is *not* the same as merely becoming a Western mystic or an Eastern yogi. After all, there is a reason *why* Buddha was asked if he was the coming "savior of the world," and he said "NO." There is a reason *why* Muhammed told of a vision he had wherein he saw all the great elders and masters of the past, but he said that Jesus was at the top of this pyramid. There is a reason *why* all the ascended masters refer to Jesus (aka Sananda) as the "Master of all masters." **There is a reason *why* all the great teachers, philosophers, healers, and prophets of the past died, and only Jesus overcame death and brought himself back to life.**

Jesus is *not* merely a "pretty good teacher" of the past. Instead, he broke the spell that evil (the ego) once had over all of humanity—even though it's taking over two thousand years for the effects to fade away. **He was the first to *completely* remember that he was the Christ and he is now assisting us to do the same.** Now it's up to us to accept this awakening—a process and experience that is commonly referred to as the "Second Coming of Christ."

⋙⋘

*Jesus began his journey as a human being
like all of us, but eventually became one
with God. He then agreed to return to
Earth to help others attain the same.*

–Yogananda

And for those who doubt that *this* is the time
when the old world is dying, thus making room for a
new world, they would be disputing Hopi prophecy,
Native American prophecy, the Mayan calendar (and
they were known as the planetary time-keepers), the
timeline of the Jewish Jubilees, Nostradamus, angelic
visions, Edgar Cayce, astrology, the Bible and Book
of Revelation, the visions of hundreds of mystics, the
visionary children of Fatima and Medjugorje, as well
as thousands of people who have experienced NDE's
(near death experiences) wherein they were shown
the coming changes to the world.

⋙⋘

*Behold, the darkness shall cover the earth,
and deep darkness shall cover the people; But
the LORD will arise over you, and His glory
will be seen upon you.*

–Isaiah 60:2

Those who tend to disbelieve the time we are in, are simply those who are most afraid to accept it. They might also tend to minimize the role of Jesus or of the Divine Mother. But again, this is merely an expression of their fear of the inevitable, which results in postponing their own awakening. The Daughters of Heaven have no reason to doubt the times in which we are living nor do they doubt the role of Christ. They know *who* they serve and *why*.

The Daughters of Heaven are here to bring peace and comfort. They are very much like human versions of the angels who appeared before humans in "days of old" with messages from God. They are like the angels who have appeared in the bedrooms of children in the middle of the night to offer comfort during challenging times.

The Daughters of Heaven might, or might not, be Christians; but if they are, they are not necessarily "Fundamental" Christians—simply because they are *not* impressed by preaching to, nor shaming others. Instead, **they are moved by authentic love, compassion, and any person or being who is a living example of the Love of God.** In fact, it could righteously and accurately be said that the Daughters of Heaven are now ready to come forth to a new level of Christ Consciousness because of, or in spite of, the old school methodology of preaching *their* version of the word of God, but were rarely, if ever, authentically in touch *with* God. They, instead, gravitate towards those who *feel* and *commune* with God—each and every day.

Some of the Daughters of Heaven are former, or current, Pagans—sometimes having been women who have been burned at the stake for their beliefs. But this terrible fate was, to them, a relief and a *worthwhile* fate that released them from a life where they were constantly being harassed and punished for honoring or worshiping the Divine Mother—in forms that were unacceptable to the "powers that be." To them, however, death was a better destiny than to be forced to conform to a false religion founded on fear and brutality.

The Daughters of Heaven *knew* that **this church could *not* be the *real* church, as it didn't feel like the Love of the Divine Mother (Holy Spirit) of God** that they experienced in their hearts. The world was made to believe that God is a masculine force, and a frightening one at that. To make matters worse, the church led people to believe that it was *indeed* the embodiment *of* God. Therefore, complete devotion and unquestionable loyalty became the law. All this accomplished was for people to learn to fear God and to fear Love.

※

Do not conform to the pattern of this world, but be transformed by the renewing of your mind. Then you will be able to test and approve what God's will is—His good, pleasing and perfect Will.

–Romans 12:2

Masculinity, like femininity, can be accessed or used properly or improperly. The ideal thing is to have an appropriate balance of both. **The use of the term "Daughters" has little or *nothing* to do with our gender. It's a reference to our soul**—which has been defined in mythology for thousands of years as being feminine. So the "Daughters" of Heaven can also be "sons," or males, but not men who excessively gravitate towards their *masculine* traits. They are males who are in touch with their heart and soul—their humble and receptive self—men who can openly serve "the Mother."

The Daughters of Heaven are *not* to be confused with those who misinterpret the concept of being "goddesses." The term "goddess" means many different things to many different people. But for some, the term connects with ancient mythology when gods and goddesses *controlled* the Earth from the heavens above OR the ones that once lived *on* Earth. For example, some of **today's Daughters of Heaven were the "goddesses of charity," known as the "Graces" in mythology.** The Graces are the goddesses of charm, beauty, creativity, goodwill, and nature. They are considered to be the daughters of Zeus and an Oceanid named Euronyme. They were also attendants of Aphrodite, and were known to join the "Muses" in singing and dancing.

The Daughters of Heaven are also found in Greek mythology in relation to the goddess, Eileithyia, who was generally depicted as a woman wielding a torch/lantern, symbolizing that she is a Lightworker, and/or with her arms raised in the air, a symbol of being a Daughter of Heaven who humbly calls down the Presence of God. Eileithyia was also well-known as the "goddess of childbirth," "protector of the newborn," and the "goddess of helpfulness."

While there is certainly a time and place for some women to stand in *their* power and strength, **the Daughters of Heaven choose instead to stand in the**

Power and Strength of *God*. And in this choice to be *humble*, they are made *strong*. The three greatest role models and examples of the life, humility, and consciousness of a Daughter of Heaven are Mother Mary, Mary Magdalene, and Thecla. All three of these amazing women were baptized by the Holy Spirit and anointed by Christ Jesus.

The Daughters of Heaven always felt an unusual, almost familiar, relationship with Jesus or one of the three female archetypes previously mentioned. They would sometimes be seen as "dreamers," or would be judged as "odd" because they spoke about Jesus as though he was a *friend*. They may have spoken about angels as though they could regularly communicate with them—because they *could*! **Although it was/is often challenging to live among dense human beings, this was all a part of their training.**

These Daughters of Heaven were/are also able to recognize various signs of their identity—similar to those who have a membership to an exclusive group. These symbols included phrases like: "The Sacred Heart of Jesus" or "The Immaculate Heart of Mary." Terms like these seem familiar *not* just because they may have heard such terms spoken in various books or religions, but because **they were terms of activation—phrases that were planted in their mind like "time released" downloads.** And each of these downloads were given to them for the following reasons: 1) To uplift them and support them in their work in a dense world. 2) To raise their level of vibration so that they are more prepared for higher and higher vibrations and downloads— similar to having updates downloaded onto a computer or phone.

The Daughters of Heaven are a great example of the phrase "The last shall be first and the first shall be last"—because they don't need to stand out. They are gradually learning that who they *really* are is *always* enough, which means they no longer need to *strive* to be seen. They often prefer a humble role, and this allows them to be lifted to the highest position of spiritual attainment for any human being.

Unfortunately, **some of the Daughters of Heaven will still slip out of their position of Christ Consciousness if/when they attempt to step into a position of power and control.** Again, their greatest gift is in humble service, more so than in leadership—although they are sometimes leaders.

However, even if they *do* choose to shift into a more powerful role, wherein they assert their own power and strength, it doesn't necessarily mean they have completely become controlled by their ego. They might simply be switching into the role of being the more assertive Lightworker, and Lightworkers clearly have an important role in the awakening of humanity.

Another one of the most common setbacks for the Daughters of Heaven is when they confuse the commitments made in previous lifetimes (e.g. as a priest or nun), with their current commitment to being filled with the Spirit. But they will know the difference, and more easily navigate this potential trap, when **they recognize and refuse the call to be "religiously rigid" versus "spiritually inspired." One is *doing*, and the other is *being*.**

Although the "inner nun" might feel compelled to wear dark clothes and dutifully refrain from many natural human activities (prosperity, affection, and so on), the Daughters of Heaven are learning to answer the call from the Holy Spirit to do *whatever* they need to do to lift the spirit of others. They might feel inspired to laugh, smile, or dance. They might also feel called to withdraw into deep communion with God. Whatever the case, **their personal mantra is "How can I be truly helpful today?"**

A Daughter of Heaven goes through stages of accepting this title or role. This includes accepting one's value—which generally has two major stages—each of these having their own sub-stages. The two major stages are: 1) Healing traumas and abuses that created low value and low self-worth; 2) Accepting new levels of value—romantically, financially, intellectually, spiritually, and so on.

To awaken the Daughter of Heaven within, means to awaken one's heart center—which is why so many women (and men) have described supernatural sensations igniting in their heart when they hear about this group of dedicated souls and the role that they play through their dedication to God.

No eye has seen, no ear has heard, and no mind has imagined what God has prepared for those who love Him.

–1 Corinthians 2:9

A Daughter of Heaven feels compelled—sooner or later—to release her past. She chooses to release past addictions or any other form of self-abuse. She finds herself no longer the victim of previous heartbreak, nor a victim of previous abuses or circumstances. Any perpetrators of past traumas eventually are seen as being a faint memory and no longer holding power over her life. The attention of a Daughter of Heaven is far more focused on the love and light in the *present*, than it is on the pain and darkness of the *past*. They know that the people from their past are not related to their newfound priority of connecting with Spirit, and they are now seen and released for what they really *are*—valueless. After all, why would anybody in their right mind cling to a valueless chunk of rock, if they had before them, a pot of gold?

Although the Daughters of Heaven are only recently being activated in this *present* generation, they are referred to in the oldest mythological story of all time—the story of Sophia—which explains the history (her–story) of the human soul that came into the Earth and became trapped in the amnesia of her true identity. Her beloved spiritual brother—the Christ—came to her and brought her home. But the proverbial final chapter of her story is that instead of simply returning home, to Heaven, she remained on the Earth to help others in *their* awakening from their spiritual coma or amnesia.

For *this*, the Daughters of Heaven can be referred to as the "Living Saints of God."

ANSWERING THE CALL

Most of the Daughters of Heaven might very well feel an affinity with many of the descriptions and definitions shared in this material, but they still might not have *completely* stepped into this lifestyle. This book is their call to do so.

Furthermore, instead of assuming that you are *not* a Daughter of Heaven because you haven't yet stepped into the embodiment of the descriptions given throughout this material, it's better to know that **most of the Daughters of Heaven have thus far only had feelings, suspicions, and a few pieces of the puzzle . . . that is, until now.** Now the pieces are coming together, and they will soon realize *who* they are and *what* they are here to do.

There will of course be *some* women (and men) who would like to automatically assume that *they* are Daughters of Heaven when in fact, their ego might be tricking them. **A person *cannot* be a Daughter of Heaven simply because they *insist* that they are**—especially if they only feel an affinity to a small percentage of the relevant characteristics.

They might instead be a Lightworker—which is a lot like a Daughter of Heaven—but they are *not* the same. The key to knowing where we really stand, is in the humility within the soul and not in the assertion of the head.

Those who truly *are* Daughters of Heaven, are hearing the call to assist in the Grand Awakening and most have already incarnated to do their part. Now, **all they need to do is *answer* the call** and make the choice to continue to nurture their relationship with Jesus, Mother Mary, and the Divine Mother. **They simply need to let the Holy Spirit know that they are now ready, and are making the conscious choice to awaken, and to begin helping others to awaken**—mostly by their grace-filled presence.

You need to hear the truth about yourself as frequently as possible, because your mind is so preoccupied with false self-images.

–A Course in Miracles

For those who may have not *already* dedicated lifetimes to living this lifestyle, but desire to do so, **it would mean taking a crash course with the Holy**

Spirit, as well as making major changes in one's life and lifestyle. This is certainly an option that is available to all. But, as the old saying goes, "Be careful what you ask for."

Answering this call now, but without having lived a life of dedication before, would first entail making a heart-felt appeal to the Divine Mother, asking to be made into a Daughter of Heaven, followed by living according to that lifestyle. The rest will likely fall into place.

CHAPTER FOUR

Characteristics of the Daughters of Heaven

AM I A DAUGHTER OF HEAVEN?

The characteristics of the Daughters of Heaven are numerous, as might be expected when it comes to describing these most unique souls. In general, however, **the Daughters of Heaven are not so much defined by how they look, nor by their chosen life or lifestyle, as much as by how they think, act, and feel.**

The external expressions of a Daughter of Heaven may vary *tremendously* because the different manifestations of the Holy Spirit can vary tremendously—and **the Daughters of Heaven are manifestations (or embodiments)** *of* **the Divine Mother**—or Holy Spirit.

It can generally be said, however, that the Daughters of Heaven tend to take care of their physical and emotional needs, but without being intensely obsessed about them. They prefer casual, loose-fitting clothing rather than a rigid type of apparel, such as business suits or high heels. And **they might very-well be found to enjoy wearing scarves**—even if they don't know why. These scarves might be worn on their arms and shoulders, or even over their head. When worn over their head, it is a symbolic statement that they want to keep God *in*, and the world *out*.

The following is a list of many of the common characteristics of the Daughters of Heaven. You might relate to *all*, *some*, or *none* of these. If you feel an affinity to *all* of these characteristics, great! Then you will clearly feel right at home with this material. If you feel absolutely *no* affinity to *any* of these, then you probably wouldn't even feel drawn to reading this material. If you feel an affinity to *some* of these characteristics, but also feel as though you *lack* some of them—or haven't been living up to the presumed lifestyle of a Daughter of Heaven—there's no need to feel discouraged. Instead, just **look within your heart to see if you *now* feel the** pieces coming together, and that you are hearing (to a far greater extent) the call to serve God and the Heavenly Host. In other words, if you aren't sure, maybe it's because the seeds are only now being planted. Your job then, would be to water and feed them into maturity.

However, if a majority of these characteristics seem familiar, or seem to fit your personality (and/or lifestyle), then you are indeed likely to be one of the Daughters of Heaven. But, if there were only one characteristic that we could use to determine if we are a Daughter of Heaven, it is "a humble devotion to God"—or to any part of the Divine Trinity, including devotion for the embodiments of the Divine, in the form of Jesus and Mother Mary.

It might easily be assumed that being one of the Daughters of Heaven is a grand label or achievement, and in some ways, it is. But it's also important to consider the challenges of being such a soul. They are often individuals who never felt like they fit in. It's also common for them to be single, and to have long periods of time abstaining from sex—not necessarily because they have sexual wounds or inhibitions, but because of their high levels of sensitivity and integrity, and a spiritual maturity that will not allow them to settle for shallow versions of intimacy—which is really not intimate at all.

Although it is said here that many of the Daughters of Heaven are known to be healers or are known to be affectionate or are known to be have a history of devotionalism in previous lifetimes, it doesn't necessarily mean that this is the way it is for *all* of them. These are merely general guidelines that are *mostly* true and applicable for these lovely souls.

SPECIFIC TRAITS & REMINDERS

Affection: The Daughters of Heaven are not prudes. They are very often affectionate—even more affectionate than those who think of themselves as open-minded and free spirited. For example, there are those in a "New Thought" church who think of themselves as loving, and they might be seen exchanging hugs with other attendees. This is true as well for the Daughters of Heaven, except that they might also be seen kissing their friends on the cheeks, or even on the lips. Jesus was also described in some of the "lost gospels" as sometimes kissing his friends—including Mary Magdalene—on the lips when they greeted each other. This was not an act of romance and partnership, as some people would lead their followers to believe. The translations from the original languages were saying that the act of kissing each other on the lips simply meant that Jesus was "sharing the same breath" with these friends—which meant that they were sharing the same *spirit*—the Loving Spirit of God.

Almost Angels: The Daughters of Heaven are nearly as close to being embodied angels as one can be. This is not because they are "special" in some way, nor is it because they are "ethereal," as much as it is because angels are constantly loving and praising God no matter *what* is going on or *who* is around them. The Daughters of Heaven are very much the same way; they are often in a state of love, praise, and gratitude to all Aspects of God. Also, similar to angels, they have a tendency to embody love, forgiveness, purity of heart, and humility. But, above all else, they aspire to be a servant of God.

<hr>

To the pure in heart, all things are pure.

–Titus 1:15

Celibacy: Being detached from their sexuality and their body tends to reflect some of their former programs related to vows of celibacy. The *guilt* related to this comes from *past* programs and is not meant for the Daughters of Heaven in the *present*. Although celibacy and devotion to God, or Jesus, have been chosen by many as statements of their loyalty and devotion, they were never meant to be taken too literally. The Daughters of Heaven were merely being asked to make God their first Love— their first priority. It was never meant to be about "killing all other desires," nor as a command to refrain from human intimacy. They were never asked to commit their romantic needs *only* to God. It meant simply that their relationship with God—and their spiritual path—should be their *first* priority—even *above* romantic partnerships. In other words, they need not forgo their spiritual principles just because they're having a human, romantic relationship.

Channels: The Daughters of Heaven are the most likely candidates to become "integrated channels"— which is the *highest* form of channeling. This level of channeling rejects the tendency to channel "outside" beings, and instead encourages us to channel the Divine Mother (or Holy Spirit) within, and to *become* that which we are channeling. In this case, we—like Jesus—become *one* with the Holy Spirit by *channeling* the Holy Spirit. This is not the same as most channels in the world today who seem content to channel whatever entity or energy that happens to be passing by. Instead, the Daughters of Heaven choose to be channels of the Holy Spirit— which is also a way of becoming ONE with God—a process that progresses over time.

Countenance: The Daughters of Heaven are different from other people on (or off) the spiritual path—partly attributed to the light that emanates from within them, that often appears as a sweetness and glow to their face, as well as a look of peace and contentment.

---

*The peace of God, which surpasses
all understanding, guards their hearts
and minds in Christ.*

–Philippians 4:7

Creativity: The Daughters of Heaven are usually creative, or at least appreciate creativity. But this connection with creativity also tends to make them highly sensitive—sometimes overly sensitive—

which can lead to a life with more suffering than is necessary. Being sensitive, combined with deep devotion, makes the Daughters of Heaven the best candidates for being inspired and wonderfully artistic in some form. They often write songs or poems and might also like to paint items in their house, or perhaps develop a landscape or garden.

Dealing with the Past: The Daughters of Heaven have to make it a point to re-program much of the negativity that has been fed to them throughout their life. They have to accept and own that there's nothing "wrong" with them and that they are Children of God in whom God is well pleased. Also, no matter what type of relationship they may have had with their biological parents, they are learning to accept their Father and Mother God as their True Parents.

Death & Ascension: Once the Daughters of Heaven pass over, very few of them will have to incarnate again. At their passing, they are literally promoted to the role of living angels in the age soon to come. It will actually be more like their ascension, at which point they will be called "Holy Daughters of Heaven." When the average person passes away, they usually are greeted by those whom they most loved, which for them, usually means deceased family members. When the Daughters of Heaven pass away, they too are greeted by those whom they most loved, which not too surprisingly, means being greeted by Jesus, Mother Mary, and the highest of angels.

***

*I am with you always, even until
the end of time.*

–Jesus

Diet & Health: While Lightworkers might exercise and eat a healthy diet, the Daughters of Heaven tend to call the Presence of God into everything they do and into everything they eat. They don't work so hard to make things Holy. Instead, they acknowledge, and give thanks for, the holiness that *already* exists within all things—including their food and the present moment. Nevertheless, they *do* seem more attracted to fresh foods—including fruits and vegetables.

Digestion & Anxiety: The Daughters of Heaven know that they came from a dimension of peace and love into a dimension of fear and pain, which causes them various forms of inner conflict and anxiety that can have significant, detrimental effects on their digestion and health. They *know* they long for something profound—even if they know not what it is. But, as they come to discover the truth of who they *are*, and what they are here to *do*, the body's systems tend to calm down. But still, they are often sensitive souls, which means they might continue to struggle with certain sensitivities.

———

Peace. Be still, and know that I am God.
–Psalm 46:10

Eden: The Daughters of Heaven are beginning to awaken to the fact that the old world really *is* dying, making way for Heaven on Earth—Eden. Knowing this is occurring, they are stepping into the destiny given to them by God to be as midwives, helping to birth our new world. They will soon shift from being "Lights on Earth" to being "Stewards of Eden."

———

Since we are receiving a kingdom that cannot be shaken, let us be thankful.
–Hebrews 12:28-29

Egos: The Daughters of Heaven still have egos and personalities, but they are learning to take responsibility to heal such character traits, while not obsessing on their shortcomings. Instead, they are learning to stay focused on their devotion to God. They will practice making an apology and making amends wherever and whenever it's needed. But they can then move on and say, in a state of total surrender, "I am as God Created me; I will to be the Christ on Earth."

~~~

Let no hurtful words proceed out of your mouth, but instead, speak words of peace and love, that it may minister grace unto the hearers.

–Ephesians 4:29

Empaths: The Daughters of Heaven are usually highly sensitive, often trying to discover the true meaning of being empathic—which is really more about objectively loving and caring about others than it is about taking on the issues of others.

Employees of God: The Daughters of Heaven specifically serve God, the Divine Mother and Jesus, which might sound like the role of Lightworkers, but it's different. Lightworkers serve humanity by bringing all people to God. The Daughters of Heaven serve God by graciously bringing God's Spirit to humanity. Some fulfill the role of both.

Faith & Devotion: The Daughters of Heaven have levels of faith and devotion towards God that few people have in this world. They trust what they *know* and *know* what they trust.

Faith is to live by an inner knowing and believing, not by the evidence of seeing nor any other external senses.

–2 Corinthians 5:7

Friendships: Similar to *partnerships*, the Daughters of Heaven sometimes find friendships to be few and far between. This is not to say that they don't have *any* friends. It's just that if they *do*, they are usually tight, healthy, and mutually respectful friendships. In fact, their friends are sometimes also Daughters of Heaven. But once again, they are growing in their devotion to God, and to living a life of greater self-worth—leaving no room for *false* or *shallow* friendships. Instead, they insist on having *good* friendships or *none* at all.

⚜

*If we walk in the light, as he is in the light,
we have fellowship one with another.*

–1 John 1:7

Grounded: The Daughters of Heaven can feel the memory of Heaven or Eden in their souls and in their bones. This memory creates a longing to return to Eden—to a place of safety, beauty, and peace. Although this longing is understandable, it can result in not being present and grounded enough—which can result in being accident prone OR in being taken advantage of—due to *not* seeing what's happening around them. The Daughters of Heaven, therefore, have to work a little harder than some people to be fully present and/or grounded.

Healers: Given their sensitivity level and their commitment to shining God's Loving Presence, it should come as no surprise that the Daughters of Heaven are often healers, counselors, and the like. They might share these talents as a licensed career or possibly as a side hobby. Either way, they will find that their work and its effectiveness come very naturally. All they have to do now, is remember to dedicate and sanctify each session to the miraculous power of Jesus, the Holy Spirit, and/or Mother Mary. And it's important to remember that we are not asking the Divine to "fix" our client's body, nor any part of their material life. Instead, we are asking that they be *filled*, or *flooded* with the Holy and Perfect Presence of God—where all such issues, illnesses, and challenges do *not* (cannot) exist.

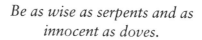

Be as wise as serpents and as innocent as doves.

–Jesus

Humility & Holding Space: Just as the Divine Mother has been "holding space" for all of Her Children since the beginning of time, so too are the Daughters of Heaven holding space for the Divine to be awakened within all of God's Children. This might be accomplished through acts of healing work, counseling, being a good parent, listening to the needs and issues of others, or simply holding space through silent prayer. Most of the Daughters of Heaven have very little need to be "seen." They are *not* as interested in becoming popular figures in the world of spirituality and self-help as they are in holding space and being of service to God—their first love and first priority.

***

Do nothing out of selfish ambition or vain conceit. Rather, in humility value others above yourselves, not looking to your own interests but each of you to the interests of the others. In your relationships with one another, have the same mindset as Christ Jesus: Who, being in very nature God, did not consider equality with God something to be used to his own advantage; rather, he made himself nothing by taking the very nature of a servant, being made in human likeness.

–Philippians 2:3-7

Intuitive: The Daughters of Heaven are highly intuitive but they are constantly having to learn lessons about trusting themselves. Also, being so sensitive, they have to take care not to pick up on the feelings of others when they are not being called on by Spirit to do so. This issue tends to dissipate when they develop better boundaries and strengthen their auric field—the "Armor of the Lord."

Judgment & Forgiveness: The Daughters of Heaven would, in no way, live a life of persistent judgmental attitudes, nor would they be interested in criticizing the lives of others. They are, instead, at peace within themselves, which tends to erase the desire to be in *conflict* with others or to *control* others. The Daughters of Heaven are clearly evolved enough to know the worthlessness of judging and the value of forgiveness and therefore, live accordingly.

Bear with each other and forgive one another if any of you has a grievance against someone. Forgive as the Lord Jesus forgave you.

–Colossians 3:13

Lifestyle: They aren't always "straight" nor gay, meat eaters nor vegans, bankers nor artists. Therefore, they cannot be identified so easily. Instead, they can be recognized by their consistent decision to be spontaneously guided and inspired as to what to say, what to wear, what to eat, and so forth. They prefer to be Guided as to the best life or lifestyle for them in the moment. In other words, a Daughter of Heaven is led more by inspiration that comes from the heart of the Divine Mother, than by the compulsions and dictates of their ego OR from the ego of others.

Money & Material Things: The Daughters of Heaven are sometimes former nuns who have taken "vows of poverty." They are also sometimes individuals with past or current wealth and/or fame. In either case, the Daughters of Heaven are learning now, that in order to truly *have* anything, they must first learn how to *give*. Therefore, they are constantly expanding their desire to give and share *whatever* they can, *whenever* they can. They are learning that they need neither *avoid* money nor become *attached* to it. Instead, they allow themselves to receive from God's rich Abundance, take care of their needs and desires, and then, to share these riches—riches of love, happiness, prayers, or wealth.

Nature Lovers: The Daughters of Heaven tend to love life and its beauty. They love animals, colors, flowers, and flower essences. They not only thrive in environments of flowing water, greenery, fresh air, and wildlife, they also love the less visible, etheric side of nature. They know that the etheric world of fairies and sylphs is real, and is an extension of the Divine Mother and the Earth Mother. In fact, a large number of these blessed Daughters once lived in the etheric realm, some even lived as gods and goddesses and/or as *children* of the gods and goddesses, as we find recorded in Greek mythology. But as much as they love the beauty of the physical and etheric nature in the *outer* world, the Daughters of Heaven know that even the *greatest* beauty of Earth doesn't compare in the *slightest*, to the visions beheld in the Nature of God.

Nurturers: They are nurturers—spiritual mothers— even if they have *no* experience with raising children— because they are devoted to being expressions of the *Divine* Mother. The Daughters of Heaven find themselves, quite naturally, stroking the forehead of someone who is sad or weary, or consoling someone who has experienced a loss. This is simply second nature to them because they are mothers and/or nurturers.

Partnerships & Relationships: The Daughters of Heaven *love* love, and yet are willing to go without romantic love *if* that "love" is not founded upon *spiritual* love. This means that they honor themselves and their sanity more than the experience of shallow levels of romance. There is no longer the option of settling or bargaining. Following such guidelines is how they assure themselves of having the highest possible version of relationships. In the meantime, they often label themselves as "single and unavailable."

Delight yourself in the Lord, and He will give you the desires of your heart.

–Psalm 37:4

The Daughters of Heaven are the first group of individuals to have begun training on the real purpose of relationships—which frankly, makes this part of their lives one of the most challenging. Relationships were *never* supposed to be destined for two or more people to get together to become codependent. Relationships were *never* supposed to be simply about mating for procreation, nor about pairing up with someone else to avoid being alone. Relationships were *never* supposed to be about two or more people because there *are* no two or more people.

All the world, and all the bodies living in the world are actually a *hologram*—mirroring how we feel inside about our relationship with God and with ourselves. Relationships were, therefore, only ever meant to serve two *real* purposes: 1) To see our issues and lessons reflected back to us so that we might choose to heal such issues. 2) To receive the gifts from having *healed* our issues and *learned* our lessons. If we don't see and heal our issues and lessons, we will not witness or experience any of these gifts that are available to us. If, on the other hand, we achieve the healing and advancement from these two steps, we experience what is known as a "Healed and Holy Relationship"—romantic or otherwise.

Achieving Holy Relationships is, and always has been, the one and only purpose and goal of our relationships. To know this, then removes the standard dramas and false roles we play in relationships—which the average person perceives as potentially boring. The truth is, however, this makes our relationships Holy and Sacred— Blessed by God. As we heal our perception of our relationships, we too are then healed. What we once perceived as *two* individuals—liking or disliking each other—becomes *one* person (the Holy Christ) loving *all* others—which is then reflecting their love for God and themselves.

The Daughters of Heaven are now becoming committed to having Holy Relationships with all souls and all beings. This will often make them seem, and feel, non-committal and disinterested in partnerships. In truth, however, they are *indeed* committed, but only to a higher order of relationships—*Holy* Relationships—filled with true love.

Past Lives: A large percentage of the Daughters of Heaven have lived at *least* one lifetime as a nun, a priest, a monk, or on some similar path. Ironically, they also may have incarnated as those persecuted by those *very* same religious authorities. This latter example would include the wise ones of the past who were misjudged as witches, or viewed as being "too odd or different," causing them to hide away in order to feel safe. In either case, there was a devotion to God. However, since there was no *conscious* awareness of the Daughters of Heaven in previous lifetimes, people just did the only thing they knew to do, which usually meant gravitating toward *some* path of devotion that they could believe in—even *if* the one they chose was at odds with other, more acceptable groups.

This is by no means to suggest that *all* nuns, priests, and so forth are currently Daughters of Heaven, but it *is* accurate to say that the Daughters of Heaven often incarnated into a life where they chose a life or lifestyle that seemed the most religious or spiritual at the time. But *now*, their time has come to emerge as a "collective" and to feel the safety of God all around them while they do the work for which they were once judged.

Peace: They love peace and are natural peace-makers. They often know how to mediate arguments between others, and yet they are still learning to trust themselves enough to own this talent of theirs. But because they love peace and love to *manifest* peace, they make great spiritual counselors and/or mediators—personally or professionally.

Personality: The Daughters of Heaven are usually very passive, which is a concept that might even anger some women (or men) to read. This merely confirms that such a person who gets triggered by this has unhealed wounds and inaccurate opinions about healthy passivity and would, by default, NOT be a Daughter of Heaven—although they might still be a Lightworker. In contrast, the Daughters of Heaven tend to be at peace, having very little to prove or fight for. A Daughter of Heaven is passive, receptive, and at peace with having their type of personality and state of being.

◦◦◦

Make every effort to live in peace with everyone and to be holy; without holiness no one will see the Lord. See to it that no one falls short of the grace of God and that no bitter root grows up to cause trouble and defile many.

–Hebrews 12:14

Predicting the Future of Earth: The Daughters of Heaven have experienced lifetimes as oracles, guides, and healers—like the tribal "wise-women." So, it's quite natural for them to have clairvoyant abilities. Also, these loving beings enjoy a natural relationship with the Divine Mother and Earth Mother—an incredible relationship that has been nurtured for many lifetimes.

In the same way that wildlife is naturally in such an attuned relationship with the Earth that it can tell an earthquake is coming (long before its rumblings), the Daughters of Heaven are also capable of knowing in advance, events that are coming to the Earth, now and in the future. In fact, the time will come when this particular group will be so attuned to the Earth that they will be able to tell every previous *and* future experience in the Earth's geology. But, it will take a little more time for them to develop this level of trust with the inner Voice of the Divine Mother *and* with their ability to remain at peace, when seeing some of the cataclysmic events of the past and future.

They know that "time," as we understand it, is running out for the human race. Humans fear this because they are not in control of the timelines, nor the outcome. The Daughters of Heaven, on the other hand, are quite optimistic about this because they know that soon, everyone will return to Eden—a higher dimensionality of Christ Consciousness.

I have told you these things, so that in me you may have peace. In this world you will have trouble. But take heart! I have overcome the world.

–Jesus

Priorities: Even people who seem to be dedicated to their spiritual path often fail to have their priorities straight—putting so many mundane facets of their life above their relationship with God. Unlike those others on the spiritual path, the Daughters of Heaven don't focus so much on *external* matters—including family, work, and romance—or even on becoming "enlightened," as much as they do on accepting that their spirit and life are in God's Hands. They focus on becoming closer to God, and know that all else will then fall into place. Lightworkers focus on using various means to make the world a better place; the Daughters of Heaven focus on bringing the Presence of God *to* the world, knowing that only *this* will bring about the highest and greatest changes.

~∞~

Fortunate is the one who seeks after truth. When they find it, no one can disturb their peace.

–The Book of Thomas the Contender

Self Forgiveness: When they believe they have fallen short, the Daughters of Heaven are now learning to forgive themselves more quickly than most other people. But due to their heightened state of sensitivity, the Daughters of Heaven *still* tend to be a bit too hard on themselves—especially during the early stages of awakening to their true identity and their true purpose.

———

I have been crucified and have arisen. It is no longer my former self who lives, but Christ who lives in me. The life I now live—even in the flesh—I live by faith in Christ who loves me and the Christ that I AM.

–Galatians 2:20

Sexuality: Many of the Daughters of Heaven are learning to respect themselves enough to tell a lover that before their bodies can be touched, their hearts and souls have to be touched. They are fed-up with settling for less-than-healthy relationships. And when it comes to unhealthy sexual partners, they often abstain from any further sexual activity, which might lead them to assume that their sex life is stalled or is completely over. However, as they heal from such past wounds, they can prepare to embrace their sexual self in a healthier way—in the right time and with the right person—if they choose. This could take on a new form of sexuality, such as being gay, being straight, being solo with one's sexuality, or even taking on the form of enjoying intimacy and affection with friends *without* being fully sexual. The change referred to here is about balance.

The Daughters of Heaven are *not* prudes, but they can often come across as being quite "conservative." In truth, many of them would prefer a world where they could enjoy dancing naked under the stars or a waterfall or walking naked in a forest, but they can't seem to find the right place and time to allow such wild abandon. So when it comes to sexuality, the Daughters of Heaven need only *one* thing: to learn to step into their sensual body or share a sexual experience without sacrificing their spiritual and/or psychological health and integrity.

<hr />

We are not trying to externally please people, but rather seek to please God, who knows our hearts.

–1 Thessalonians 2:4

Vibrating, Shaking & Other Similar Sensations: Since around the year 2020, there has been an increasing number of cases of people feeling sensations, such as vibration running through their bodies. In many cases, this is a neurological response to the increasing vibration of the planet. This shaking that occurs in the nervous system might feel awkward or even overwhelming at times, but it's something a person can possibly get used to and can wrap their head around. But when a person's *energy-systems* (i.e. aura, chakras, meridians, etc.) become activated, it's a whole new ballgame.

At this point, there are internal activities going on that might either be too *subtle* to feel, or they might be too *surreal* to cope with. Whatever the case, the best means of dealing with such sensations is to remain calm and centered and prayerfully call upon the Holy Spirit to be our Guide through any of these types of activations or processes. Also, it's wise to become more "grounded" by doing physical exercises (e.g. working the hips and legs), eating grounding foods (e.g. red meats and/or below-ground veggies), listening to grounding music (e.g. tribal and/or deep drumming), and doing some grounding breath-work and meditations (e.g. slow breathing, visualizing drawing a cord from the navel center/chakra downward to the center/core of the Earth).

FIVE WAYS TO NURTURE A CLOSER RELATIONSHIP WITH GOD

The Daughters of Heaven are unique among the average human being or the average Lightworker, in that they continually walk in the Light of the Lord—not in a religious sense (with mere words and/or rituals and ceremonies)—but with humility, devotion, and most importantly, their personal relationship with God (in any form). This profound connection is founded on their sincere love for God and their daily, simple practice of communicating with God—all day long.

- Start each day by asking for the Holy Spirit, or Jesus, to be your Guide throughout the day. Also end each day by giving thanks for their Presence throughout the day.
- Read books and watch videos that encourage a healthier lifestyle and a positive perspective of God.
- Practice various kinds of prayer and meditation throughout the day. These can range from traditional prayers to casual prayers.
- Practice communion with God throughout each day—meaning to converse with Jesus, Mother Mary, or the Holy Spirit—as though

they are right there in the room with you. The conversation can be about the deepest things or the most mundane things, but try to make it as valuable to your greater good as is possible.

- Drop all perception about God being intense, judgmental, dissatisfied with you, or even being remotely disinterested in you or the improvement of your life or needs—be they material, emotional, or psychological needs. Instead, develop a regular practice of seeing God as only ever having gentle, loving, and caring thoughts about you.

CHAPTER FIVE

The Daughters of Heaven & the Divine Mother

ANCIENT ORIGINS OF THE DIVINE MOTHER

The Hebrew people were once *matriarchal* but later shifted to become more of a *patriarchal* society. This is why **the Holy Spirit was originally perceived as being synonymous with the Divine Mother.** But, as cultures changed and religions grew more powerful (becoming aggressive and hyper-masculine), the view of God shifted towards a masculine tone. In truth, however, the Holy Spirit was, and is, more accurately seen and experienced as the "Mother Aspect of God."

This Divine/Universal Mother (or Holy Spirit) is also known as the Holy Shekinah, which is the Hebrew name for the part of God that "dwells here with us." Kabbalistic Jews call Her Binah—part of the upper Trinity of the Kabbalistic tree. Binah has two aspects: 1) "The Higher Mother." 2) "The Lower Mother." These two aspects are collectively referred to as Imma—similar to *mamma* or "The Mother." Classical Jewish texts state that "an extra measure of Binah (the Divine Mother) was given to women," which is why **it seems easier or more natural for women (than men) to connect *with* the Divine Mother.**

The Divine Mother (Holy Spirit) of God is known by many other (and similar) names including "She," "Shekinah," "Shingonshu," "Shakti," and "Shiva" (even though She-va is a male deity). The Shekinah of the Israelites is fairly similar to the "Shakti" of the Hindu, and the Gnostic term "Sophia," in that all are describing the descent, or manifestation, of the Divine Mother—the real version of the Divine Feminine. Notice how often the sound of the "She" portion of this word—a female pronoun—appears in various cultures.

She is "chi"! Chi is the energy of life that is also known as orgone, life-force, or human vitality. This is the Breath of Life that comes from God; and what activates, or quickens our human life. This chi is the light that surrounds all things, and permeates all things. Chi is also pronounced "ki" or "gi," which is the root of the words "kia" or "gia," or "Gaia"— the name for Mother Earth. So again, *chi* is *She*— the Divine Mother and/or Mother Earth. When, according to the Bible, "God breathed into our nostrils the breath of life; and we then became living souls," it was describing the Divine Mother giving us life. She (or chi), is the bridge between the realm of pure energy, and the human realm of animated, physical life—the bridge between Spirit and matter. **If chi (the Divine Mother) is absent, life is also absent.**

In the West, God is more commonly known as, or related to, our *Father*. In the East, God is more commonly known as, or related to, our *Mother*. **In the Hindu tradition, the Mother Aspect of God is known as AUM**—similar to *mom* or *mum*—and AUM is considered to be the "cosmic vibration that creates the *entire* universe."

In Tibetan Buddhism, the Divine Mother is known as Quan Yin or the Dakini: "the Sky Dweller" or "Dweller of the Heavens." A Dakini may manifest in different forms: fierce, playful, intense, nurturing, peaceful, or even as a force that upsets conformity. She may appear as a human being, as a goddess, or even as a primordial force. Tibetan Buddhists believe that *all* women are some type of Dakini manifestation.

In Hinduism, the Divine Mother is often known to manifest not only as any number of goddesses, but also as "Gopis," who are honored as the consorts, lovers, companions, and devotees of Krishna (Christ). They are said to have unconditional love and devotion to Krishna. But Gopis (and Dakini) are usually misinterpreted to be "servants" of the gods, rather than being seen as the unconditional *love* of the Mother being extended to *ALL* of God's Children.

God is love; and those that dwell in love dwell in God, and God in them. Herein is our love made perfect, that we may be confident of our future: because as God is, so are we.

−1 John 4:16

The ancient Zohar tells us that the Shekinah (or a Daughter of Heaven) can seem like a mother, sister, daughter, or bride. In the Talmud and the sacred teachings of the Kabbalah, it is said that a father's seed is imperceptible—just as the Presence of the Father Aspect of God is imperceptible in the material universe. This is why Yogananda said, "The Mother is closer to us than the Father." But in the mother's womb, the father's seed begins to grow and become seen and experienced. Similarly, it is the Divine Mother who makes the *universe* perceptible to us by making our beliefs perceptible to us—by manifesting them. She does this mainly so we can upgrade these beliefs to higher and higher perspectives until they match the Reality of God.

THE DIVINE MOTHER
IS ALL & IS *IN* ALL

The Divine Mother was with us when our life in this universe began. She walked with us through the veil between Heaven and the material universe. And She became the womb of the universe itself in which we were born and now live. During the early Christian era, "The Secret Book of John" defined the Holy Spirit as the "Divine Mother" and the "Universal Womb."

Every atom, subatomic particle, and subatomic wave in this universe is like a cell of Her womb. But it's not like a womb that we emerge from when we experience a physical birth. It's a "cosmic womb" that is the entire universe, from which we *never* depart—that is until we are birthed as beings of Christ Consciousness back into Heaven. At that point, **the entire universe and the human race will contract back into the Light of Oneness.**

God is Light;
in God there is no darkness at all.

–1 John 1:5

The word "matter" comes from the word "mother." And **the Mother loves us so much that She shifts from being the "unlimited *Mother*" to becoming "limited *matter*," just so She can serve as a mirror of our beliefs.** She is *literally* the atomic energy behind all matter, as well as behind all materialized actions. For the average person, life is not so much an expression of the Mother living *through* us as much as it is the Mother who materializes *for* us—to mirror our thoughts and beliefs.

Again, the "Divine Mother" became "Divine Matter," the very dust that makes up our universe—including the Earth—Mother Earth. In so doing, She helps us to manifest our thoughts and beliefs in a form that represents our current issues and lessons. **She mirrors things to us so that we might choose differently, and shift our consciousness**, which would then alter our beliefs, thoughts, and behaviors.

⁓⦿⁓

The origin of heaven and earth is nameless—the Mother of all things.

–The Tao Te Ching

She will play this game with us for billions of years, if necessary, until all of Her children have acted out the very last of their ego-based thoughts and beliefs and have chosen then to surrender all such things, thus making room for something new— the thoughts and beliefs of God. **The ultimate goal then is to learn to surrender ourselves so much to *Her* that we begin materializing *Her* Will and Beliefs instead of our *own*.**

The Divine Mother took on the form of the mythological primordial forces that brought all matter into being. Then, She materialized further in the form of the feminine goddesses of mythology. Then She materialized even further as mortal women, and eventually as the nurturing (feminine) part of every person—male *or* female. If a man or woman accesses the part of themselves that knows how to "inspire and protect," they are in touch with their *masculine* side. But if they know how to love and nurture, they are in touch with their *feminine* side—a *mortal* version of accessing an *immortal* concept/consciousness.

In the sky, the "Sun"—which is the name we gave to the star in the center of our solar system—is a symbol of God. It offers life, light, and warmth to those who live in the darkness of space. And the fact that it's nearly impossible to look at the sun directly with our eyes for any length of time without causing damage to our eyes, is symbolic of us feeling as though we are unworthy of such a close connection. But the Mother chose to find another way for us to connect with the Light of the Father, by becoming the moon that can reflect the Light of God. And we can indeed look at the moon at night for as long as we desire. It's because **the moon is a symbol of the Mother, and the Mother reflects the Father—and all else for that matter.** She is a buffer and a bridge between *us* and direct contact with God, the Father.

There are people who claim that many ancient cultures (e.g. Hindu, Pagan, etc.) were/are polytheistic and that they worship idols and images of every kind—worshiping trees, rocks, stars, and critters. But the truth is, they were/are simply acknowledging the many different forms that the Divine, Mother Aspect of God takes on for us. The true masters within such groups know full-well that **they are *not* worshipping the "*thing*" so much as they are honoring the Light of the Mother *behind* that thing.**

The Divine Mother is the Divine Light *behind* all things, but She is also the manifestation *of* all things. She crystallizes so that we can see Her, and She will do so until the day we no longer use our senses and the limited mind to discern our environment. Then we will only be able to see Her as She *really* is— Pure Light. In the meantime, the *manifestation* of a thing is synonymous with the *death* of that thing— the thing that was once Pure Light. It might sound strange, but it's true. As soon as something is made manifest, it is technically a symbol *of* death, because it is perishable and capable of dying.

This is why in the Taoist and Hindu traditions, the Father is considered the "Creator of Life," and the Mother is the "Destroyer of Life." The Mother is seen as the "destroyer" for two reasons: 1) When She manifests for us, it's as though She is frozen in time and made into something limited and perishable (capable of death), as limitation is always a form of death. 2) When She convinces us to give up some old pattern of behavior or belief, the Mother will "destroy" the previous form that had us stuck, thus allowing Her to take on (create) a new form that matches our new, hopefully higher belief-systems. So, She destroys and transforms old things into new things.

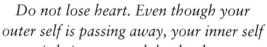

Do not lose heart. Even though your outer self is passing away, your inner self is being renewed day by day.

–2 Corinthians 4:16

The Holy Spirit, or Divine Mother, is the result of God extending Itself as Love in order to save Its Holy Children from their belief and experience of separation from God and from each other. When we, the Children of God, were descending into the universe, the Divine Mother became the Universal Womb in which to catch us when we "fell." In so doing, it was certain that, even in the illusion, we can never be separate from God.

꙳

God is Light;
in God there is no darkness at all.

–1 John 1:5

THE MOTHER AS OUR GUIDE
& COMFORTER

Again, the Divine Mother is always working with us, Her children, to help us evolve until we reach the point of returning Home—to Heaven. We can participate in Her work either *with*, or *without*, our conscious awareness. When we do so *without* having an awareness of Her assistance, we are *still* working with the Mother, because She is the only *real* power in the universe. But, without our *conscious* awareness, She can only *now* be the mirror for a person who is "lost," which manifests as greater struggles and life challenges. Such people will certainly still evolve, but at a slower pace and in a more painful way.

───❧───

Neither height nor depth, nor anything else in all creation, will be able to separate us from the Love of the Divine Mother that is in Christ Jesus, and within ourselves.

–Romans 8:39

As we learn to develop a *conscious* relationship and dependence on the Holy Spirit *and* learn to co-create a life with the Divine Mother as our *Guide*, we will experience far greater levels of awakening *and* with far less effort. In fact, **it is *only* with our *conscious* awareness of the Holy Spirit as our Guide that we can become the Christ**—the highest possible consciousness anyone can attain. That's why Jesus said, upon his departure, that he was leaving us in the hands of the Holy Spirit as our "Comforter" and "Guide."

She can be called upon at any time, and She will always answer—albeit often not in the form we expect—which is exactly why we so often fail to recognize Her work. She will assist us in improving our lives by *never* enabling our ego, nor its many disguises. She responds to our call when we faithfully call Her into any sacred space, or "yantra"—as it is called in the practices of yoga and tantra.

THE MOTHER
WHO BIRTHS THE CHRIST

Although the Divine Mother manifested the original "Immaculate Conception" by birthing us into matter, She never believed that physical form is the Truth of who we are. Instead, She maintains an Immaculate Concept (Image) of us all—seeing us as the Perfect and Innocent Christ Child. The Divine Mother sees us only as being filled with grace and never sees us as being sinful. In other words, She has *never* lost faith in us, even though we often lose faith in ourselves and in each other. So, to *have* faith in ourselves and/or each other is an attribute of the Divine Mother within us.

It is for your good that I am going away.
Unless I go away, the Comforter (Holy
Spirit) will not come to you; but as I go,
I will send the Comforter (the Divine
Mother) to you and She will give you birth.
–Jesus

Without the Mother Aspect of God, we cannot be born into the Christ that we *are* because it takes a

Holy Mother to birth a Holy Child—which is why Mother Mary had to be "Christed" enough to give birth to the Christ Jesus. And although it was his *human* mother that birthed his physical *child*-body, it was the Holy Spirit, or his *Divine* Mother, that birthed his *Christ*-body. Again, it is only the Divine Mother—God—that makes possible the birth of the Christ within us.

Jesus was the embodiment of the Holy Spirit—the Divine Mother—as was Mother Mary when she too completely surrendered her will to the Will of the Holy Spirit. So we could technically say that **although Mary was a girl, and a woman, and a mother, she was also the embodiment of the Divine Feminine, and of the Divine Mother**—the Mother Aspect of God. The Divine Mother is the one who births us *into* this universe, and She is the one that will birth us *out* of this universe, and eventually back to Heaven Itself.

The topic of the "divine feminine" is one of the most misunderstood topics of today. There are loads of teachers and authors who think that we are able to "will ourselves" into awakening our divine masculine or divine feminine selves—without the Guidance of Spirit. But what they often miss is that in order to birth *anything* significant within us, we need not assert *our* will, but rather call upon the assistance and Will of the Divine Mother.

THE DIVINE MOTHER WITHIN *US*

Both men and women of any gender and any age are capable of this and can access and nurture their connection to the Divine Mother by nurturing concepts and behaviors within themselves that have to do with love, grace, and forgiveness. When the idea of accomplishing this seems too far removed, it is evidence that we feel unworthy or incapable of accessing the Mother Aspect of God.

Our *human* mother gave us birth, and so we carry the physical genetics of our parents on Earth. But when we are "born again" of the *Divine* Mother (or Holy Spirit), we carry Her "*Spiritual* Genetics"— which are far more significant than *human* genetics could *ever* be. This is why, in the deepest part of our being, we love and appreciate everything related to the Mother.

❦

*God as Divine Mother ever watches over
Her human children . . . That is why I like
to relate to God not as the grim Deity of
some prophets, but as the Mother Divine
waiting to take all of Her children back
Home after their free-will wanderings on
the error-strewn pathways of incarnations.*

–Yogananda

The Piscean Age was the age of birthing the presence of Christ on Earth. The "new age," the Age of Aquarius (which we are in now), is an "age of *grace*"—a time of accepting the gift of grace that comes from the Divine Mother. **This current era is clearly the era of Christ Consciousness and the return to honoring our Divine Mother.**

SEVEN FACTS ABOUT THE HOLY SPIRIT

- The Holy Spirit is Available to Us All.
- The Holy Spirit is ONE with the Father and the Son/Christ.
- The Holy Spirit is the Mother that Births Our Christ Self.

- The Holy Spirit is the Mother of All Creation.
- The Holy Spirit is the Source of Higher Teachings.
- The Holy Spirit is the Ultimate Bridge.
- The Holy Spirit is the Love of God, Sent to All of God's Children to Call Us Home.

SEVEN WAYS THE HOLY SPIRIT APPEARS TO THE DAUGHTERS OF HEAVEN

1. **Synchronicity**: This is the most general way that the Holy Spirit appears to each and every person during each and every day throughout our lives. She is as close to us as our own aura—enveloping us, warming us, protecting us, and shining through us. And yet, somehow, people can still assume that She's *not* there. Just as most people do not see their own aura, they *also* do not see the Presence of the Holy Spirit. It doesn't mean She's not *there*, but it certainly confirms that they are not open to seeing and experiencing Her—at least not *yet*.

2. **Inspiration & Visions**: Most people don't realize it, but the Holy Spirit inspires us to alter our posture, to smile, paint, sing, dance, and make love. She lifts us up and makes us want to share Her Presence. She

also can appear in dreams and visions. Inspirations are Her way of appearing to us as a thought or feeling. Visions are Her way of appearing to us as visual manifestations—be it internally or externally.

3. **Channeling**: The Holy Spirit is the Voice for God and, therefore, can often take the form of messengers—for individuals or groups. She *might* use angels, light-beings, or even Ascended Masters. But Her focus is not as much on *whom* She chooses as the channel, but rather, is on *what* She chooses to channel *through* them. One facet or expression of channeling is that of speaking in tongues or speaking in light-language, but there are even more variations than these.

4. **Miracles & Healing**: The Holy Spirit is all about manifesting miracles in our lives. And one of the most significant forms this can take is the form of healing. So, just as the Divine Mother can ignite our throat center to channel *messages*, She can also ignite our hands and prayers to channel healing through us. She can even use our very *presence* to channel Her Blessings. Whatever the case, She is training the Daughters of Heaven to become "miracle workers."

5. **Kundalini**: The Divine Mother can take many forms, but one of the most powerful, yet confusing forms is that of "kundalini energy."

It's as though the Divine Mother materializes in the form of the Earth Mother and her grid systems. And since people live in a symbiotic relationship with the Earth, we *too* have grid systems (aka meridians) just as the Earth has grid systems. These meridians basically circulate life-force through our body and through the Earth's body. But they basically only channel enough life-force to keep the body alive, which means we are all "running on reserves."

But, when the *Divine* Mother activates the *Earth* Mother within us—thus also ramping up our grid systems—we basically come to life. The form this takes is *that* of the serpent energy (i.e. kundalini) at the base of the spine, rising up to the crown and igniting all of the body's meridians into a new level of activity. It's as though the meridians shift from channeling three-dimensional energy into channeling "liquid light" of the highest etheric frequency.

As beautiful as this all sounds, there is a large ratio of people who struggle with this experience because it *is* possible to awaken the kundalini prematurely, which means that "our spirit is willing, but the flesh is weak." In other words, although something happened in our consciousness that precipitated an energetic awakening, our body may *not* have been attuned adequately to be able to *handle* such new frequencies.

That's why authentic yoga practices were always a mind *and* body experience. Safety features were built into those systems. Today, people might be doing yoga as a physical exercise of the body, but without also training their mind and soul to keep up with the changes in the body. Or they might be exercising their mind, but without taking the necessary steps to help their body to keep up. In other words, the soul might activate things that the body is *not* ready for, and the body might activate things that the mind is not ready for.

6. **Energetic Orgasms**: This is *not* referring exclusively to something sensual. It's referring to an *energetic* experience, which might of course look similar to, or include, a sensual reaction. The appearance of spontaneous orgasms overlaps with the signs of kundalini awakening, but it's distinctly different because not all energy-surges result in kundalini awakenings, and not all kundalini awakenings result in energetic orgasms.

People—especially women—can be so energetically sensitive, their bodies begin to respond when they feel the Presence of God is near. It's as though the hand of God reaches into their heart and soul, and the body automatically responds.

Some people try to shut this down and shame it, while others completely surrender to it—even to the point of making a scene and using it to impress people. The healthiest response, however, is to humbly surrender to the experience, while prayerfully calling-in the Presence of God so that the Holy Spirit will assist us by only allowing an amount of shaking and jolting that we can handle, and would be most appropriate for the present moment. This latter point comes in handy when we find ourselves driving a car or holding a scalding cup of coffee.

7. **Additional Manifestations of the Holy Spirit**: The seventh, and final expression of the Holy Spirit includes the following *Gifts*, *Virtues*, and *Graces* of the Holy Spirit.

THE SEVEN TRADITIONAL *GIFTS* OF THE HOLY SPIRIT

In one respect, it could be said that there are seven commonly accepted *Gifts* of the Holy Spirit. In another respect, it could be said that She will come to us in *any* way She chooses—with no limit on *how* or how *often*. However, the seven *traditional Gifts* include the following:

- The Gift of Fortitude
- The Gift of Counsel
- The Gift of Knowledge
- The Gift of Wisdom
- The Gift of Piety
- The Gift of Understanding
- The Gift of Respect for God

THE SEVEN TRADITIONAL *VIRTUES* OF THE HOLY SPIRIT

There are also said to be seven traditional *Virtues* of the Holy Spirit, which include:

- The Virtue of Charity
- The Virtue of Faith
- The Virtue of Prudence
- The Virtue of Courage

- The Virtue of Hope
- The Virtue of Justice
- The Virtue of Temperance

THE SEVEN TRADITIONAL *GRACES* OF THE HOLY SPIRIT

Besides the *Gifts* and *Virtues* of the Holy Spirit, there are also seven *Graces*, which are recognized as follows:

- The Grace of Intuitive Insight
- The Grace of Service
- The Grace of Teaching
- The Grace of Encouragement
- The Grace of Generosity
- The Grace of Inspired Leadership
- The Grace of Forgiveness or Compassion

RITUAL OF BIRTHING PEOPLE BACK TO SPIRIT DURING DEATH

The following is a ritual wherein we call upon the Divine Mother to assist someone in making their transition during death. This is a very powerful and effective exercise, so please remember to practice it with humility and faith.

1. If a person is certain to be transitioning within hours or days, ask them (or the responsible relatives or friends) for permission to do a prayer to assist the process.

2. Visualize and ask the Divine Mother to reach her hands down through a portal above the body of the person transitioning.

3. Visualize her hands forming a womb or membrane down and around the body from the head to below the feet. Then, picture this womb as being filled with pure, radiant, and peaceful light. The person is now completely in the Hands of the Mother Aspect of God (the Holy Spirit).

4. Ask the Divine Mother to begin, if it is Her Will, the process of removing the soul from the person's body and drawing it back to Spirit.

5. Give thanks that all is well, and that the Divine Mother is gently caring for the soul of the person, as they joyfully and peacefully enter a dimension of peace and wholeness.

A PRAYER TO THE DIVINE MOTHER

*Divine Mother: For years I begged for, and craved,
the material things of this world in hopes that they
would appease my hunger. But now I have found
that my hunger is for You and You alone.
Therefore, I am surrendering all willingness to
settle for anything less than Your Divine Presence.
All else has only ever led me either to temporary
happiness or to total suffering.
Now I am beginning to understand that when I
give up everything I have, or once had, in truth, I
am giving up nothing because it has no true value.
But what I gain will be the equivalent to
everything because what I gain is You.
Nearly every pain and limitation I've ever
experienced was caused by me rejecting the gifts
You would give me, and I instead settled for the
false treasures I preferred to value.
Help me to forgive all those who have ever been a
manifestation of anything else but love.
Help me to forgive myself for every definition I
have ever attached to You other than love.
You are indeed the Love of God in my life, which
makes You the Love of my life.
No one else, and nothing else, can compare.
I ask You to help me navigate the world where*

illusions still have a temporary use.
I ask You to guide me in all human actions and
interactions.
I have been asleep and dreaming for so long that I
no longer know if I am a worm that dreams it's an
angel or an angel that dreams it's a worm.
Either way, to be asleep, and in a dream,
is not my destiny.
So I ask You to shatter both of these illusions
and bring me to a state of awakening where I
can know, instead of think; Where I can feel and
experience, instead of wish for.
Oh Divine Mother: when my life wasn't depicting
a never-ending cycle of my patterns of pain, it was
depicting my greatest fears.
I ask You now to break me free from this spell and
help me instead to see the life You lovingly desire
to reflect for me.
Teach me to be Your Presence on Earth. Teach me
to be Your reflection in the lives of all beings.
Let Your song sing through me, Your music
play through me, Your comforting nature caress
through me, and Your centeredness be placed
firmly in me.
When I walk into a room, I ask that You walk into
that room with me, through me, and as me.
And so it is!

CHAPTER 6

The Daughters of Heaven & Jesus, the Christ

DEDICATION TO THE MASTER

The Daughters of Heaven seem different from other people because, in many ways, they *are* different. They aren't presuming to be "better" than anyone else, but their priority *is* better, or higher, than the average person. They are not working to "evolve" themselves, nor are they working to change the world, as the Universal Lightworkers are doing. Instead, the Daughters of Heaven are longing to be with, and serve, their Master—Jesus—on Earth as well as in Heaven.

HOW JESUS IS UNIQUE

The Daughters of Heaven have a very unique relationship with Jesus, the Christ. The reason for this is that **the Daughters of Heaven are souls that are evolved and humble enough to recognize and honor Jesus as their Master/Teacher.** They know that he is *not* just another great teacher but is the "Teacher of teachers" and the "Master of masters."

───❦───

I am the Light of the world. Whoever walks in my Light will never again walk in darkness, but will have the Light of Eternal Life.

–Jesus

The Daughters of Heaven honor foremost their Father and Mother God, but they also respect Jesus as their elder brother who was the *first* to completely *become*, or *embody*, the Christ and is now showing the rest of us how to do the same. This is why the New Testament tells us that **we need to "put on the mind (Consciousness) of Christ."**

Jesus is, after all, unique in so many ways. **He is the only Master that has the "keys to the universe,"** giving him total power over everything, mainly because he completely understands the powerlessness of illusion—which includes everything in the material universe.

Notice how common it is for people of all faiths to have a near death experience wherein they meet Jesus. It's also common for mystics and masters—even those from Eastern traditions (e.g. Sri Ramakrishna and Paramahansa Yogananda) to honor and have *visions* of Jesus. It's not as common, however, for a Muslim to have a vision of Buddha, nor a Buddhist to have a vision of Mohammed. Jesus is a more common image in visions because he oversees the awakening of every entity in every dimension. **All the great masters in every dimension see Jesus as the supreme Master.** They do not feel the same way about *any* other teacher, nor *any* ancient god or goddess.

⌣⌣⌣

*All authority in Heaven and on earth
has been given to me.*

–Jesus

This is not to take away from the role of each of these teachers or prophets. They deserve kudos and our gratitude for teaching as they did, or for delivering people out of bondage as *Moses* did. The same goes for what Joan of Arc did for the French,

General George Patton did for the Europeans, and what Mother Theresa did for the poor and sickly. **We owe our gratitude to all great teachers, healers, and deliverers.** But each of these individuals was/is working for Jesus because the plan for our awakening and ascension is in *his* hands and no one else's.

For some people, reading or hearing about Jesus might seem *too* traditional, religious, or "old-school." But that's only because of the many unhealed wounds that were often brought about by the church "in the name of Jesus." Also, so many students and seekers on the path have allowed the average spiritual, or self-help material, to be good *enough* for them—settling for *less* and minimizing the *best*. Doing such is of no interest to the Daughters of Heaven. They know that Jesus was a man, but he was the *first* man to completely remember that he was the Christ—a part of God.

It all comes down to this: Christ Consciousness is the highest level of consciousness that can be reached—not because it's an actual attainment of some kind—but because it's the *Consciousness* of who we *really* are. It's the name of our Divinity. Who in their right mind would want to dispute or resist this?

JESUS: A TRUE PORTRAIT

The *Jesus* we have been told about by various religions and theologians barely resembles the real Jesus. But the essentials are similar: Jesus was born to be the Christ; he taught all those who would listen to him, and he performed numerous miracles for those who had the faith—and even for some who didn't. Jesus was eventually arrested, tortured, and crucified until dead. Then he resurrected—coming back to life—breaking the grip of "sin" and death in the greatest way possible.

God will wipe away all tears from their eyes; and there will be no more death, neither sorrow, nor crying, neither shall there be any more pain, for the former signs of limitation will be gone forever. And all things will be restored to Light.

–Revelation 21:4-5

In the Old Testament, we are told that death is the result of sin. Therefore, **by overcoming death, Jesus was proving that sin—the cause of death—is an illusion and has no real power.** He was making a statement that *present* love—not *past* guilt—is all that really matters.

A real portrait of Jesus offers a very different story from what we find in fundamental religions. The time is at hand where **we can all now embrace and appreciate a more accurate understanding of what Jesus was really like**—which clearly explains why the Daughters of Heaven have such a real, and deep love and devotion to him.

When expanding our view of Jesus, it's important to broaden our knowledge of his physical, emotional, and spiritual being. And it helps that most sources (conventional and nonconventional) agree on several details. For example, both Edgar Cayce and Roman records agree that "Jesus was 6 feet tall, was 175 pounds, had steel-blue eyes, and that he wore a pearl gray/white seamless robe." They also agree that Jesus was "sometimes stern but also happy and had good humor."

The Roman Procurator, Pontius Pilate, and a few Roman soldiers left records that say, "His hair was long and slightly curly—past his shoulders, parted in the middle of his head and slightly shaped into a point in the back—the traditional cut for the tribe of the Nazarenes. The color of his hair seems golden at times and slightly burgundy or bronze at other times. His brow is smooth and very cheerful with a face without wrinkle or spot. His nose and mouth are faultless. His beard, the same color as his hair, not long, but divided at the chin. His features are simple and mature, his eyes are changeable and bright. He is firm in his reprimands, sweet and amiable in his admonitions, cheerful without loss of gravity. His stature is straight, his hands and arms beautiful to behold. His conversation is grave, infrequent, and modest. He is the most beautiful among the children of men."

His calm centeredness impressed some, but irritated others. Pontius Pilate and others in authority were so impressed by the authenticity and wisdom of Jesus that they described him as having "noble unction regarding a new law in the name of God who had sent him." Pilate added, "Never have I seen a sweeter or more serene countenance." He also stated that "the Nazarene was as calm as innocence itself."

These regional leaders were so impressed by Jesus that they were known to sometimes try to help or protect him from the Jewish Sanhedrin Members that were plotting to kill him. He politely declined any such help.

Although most people familiar with the story of Jesus' arrest, trial, and execution know that Pilate had reservations about condemning Jesus to death, most people still *don't* know that his hesitation came from his Celtic/Druid wife, Claudia, who was able to foresee the future. Pilate wrote that she was "Weeping and throwing herself at my feet and said to me: 'Beware. Beware, and touch *not* that man; for he is holy. Last night I saw a vision. He was walking on the water and flying on the wings of the wind. He spoke to the tempest and to the fishes of the lake; all were obedient to him. And if you condemn him, a curse of death awaits you!'" And this *did* come to pass, as Pilate was executed at the command of Caesar for his role in the crucifixion of Jesus.

When Jesus died, Pontius Pilate described the experience as follows: "There was an air of desolation and sadness. I was left alone, and my breaking heart admonished me that what was passing at that moment appertained rather to the history of the gods, than that of men. A loud clamor was heard proceeding from Golgotha, which, borne on the winds, seemed to announce an agony such as was never heard by mortal ears. Dark clouds lowered over the pinnacle of the temple, and setting over the city covered it as with a veil. So dreadful were the signs that men saw both in the heavens and on the Earth that Dionysius the Areopagite (an Athenian judge) is reported to have exclaimed: 'Either the author of nature is suffering or the universe itself is falling apart.'"

CONSCIOUS CRUCIFIXION

Despite the gruesome and painful details of the crucifixion, **Jesus never wavered in his unconditional love**—even for those who most participated in his execution. Truth be known, he knew exactly *what* he was doing, and *why* he was doing it. He knew all along who would *betray* him and who would *deny* him. And yet he loved them all. He knew his Apostles would all turn their backs on him (except for John—the Beloved), and yet, he chose them as his closest friends.

Jesus knew, that when they pierced his heart with a spear to complete the crucifixion process (and to confirm he was dead), his pure and powerful blood, containing the vibration of the Christ, poured out onto the Earth, thus releasing his Holy Liquid Light. The pure, Divine Love that was held in his heart-center flowed onto the Earth, thus anointing and purifying the Earth *itself*. **The Earth (and its** inhabitants) was, therefore, Blessed with the Christ frequency, thus preparing it for its ascension into the New, Christ Age.

What Jesus taught is beyond the greatest teachings of Lao Tzu, Buddha, Socrates, Muhammad, and many others combined. The miracles he performed far surpass those brought forth by all the greatest healers throughout time. But all of this pales in comparison to his demonstration of unconditional love for all, a level of love that he was/is teaching to us all.

The crucifixion was a symbolic gesture that told all of mankind that when people—or the world— seem to crucify us, even if we need to set boundaries or create some distance, we can *also* choose to allow our love to pour out and bring Blessings to all involved.

HE LOVED THE HELL OUT OF US

The thoughtfulness and total love that Jesus feels for all creation is also depicted in what he did *after* his crucifixion and burial—which few people know about. Jesus left the *physical* realm and entered the darkest portions of the *astral* realm—the realm or dimension where we find all of mankind's deepest emotions. This is where we typically spend some time after we depart from the *physical* world. Here we experience our *lightest* emotions (concern, care, generosity, appreciation, etc.) in the *higher* portions of the astral realm; as well as our *darkest* emotions (hate, fear, greed, resentment, regret, etc.) in the *lower* portion of the astral realm.

In the case of Jesus, he purposefully descended into the darkest recesses of the astral world—known as hell, or Hades, or Tartarus—and remained there during part of his three days in the tomb. Here, he released all the souls who were trapped, due to the old laws of guilt and punishment—causing the souls who did the worst of all "sins" or deeds, to have to suffer. Jesus, however, offered release to anyone who would accept it. Now the choice was theirs, to accept either karma or grace; judgment or forgiveness—from any and all forms of punishment. This means they could now choose to either be forgiven, and remain in the Light OR they could choose to reincarnate as a means of "clearing the slate." Whichever one they could accept and believe in most, would be the one they would experience.

All of the above describes the Jesus that the Daughters of Heaven love so dearly.

Jesus was put to death—of his body—but made alive in the Spirit. After this total awakening, he went to teach and heal the imprisoned spirits (trapped in hell) who had sinned long ago (before this new dispensation of grace). After his resurrection, Jesus Christ, rose to Heaven and is with God. The angels, authorities, and powers, are now under his authority.

–1 Peter 3:18-22

THE LORD'S PRAYER
(A New Version)

Our Father-Mother God
whose Presence is Heaven,
Sacred and Holy is Your Name.
Let Your Kingdom come,
and Your Will of Love be done,
in and through us, just as it is in Heaven.
Give us this day the fulfillment of our needs,
and teach us to forgive ourselves,
as well as others.
Lead us when we are in temptation,
and deliver us from the illusions of our ego.
For only Your Way is Loving and True,
Forever and ever—And so it is! Amen.

CHAPTER SEVEN

The Daughters of Heaven & Mother Mary

HAIL MARY: AVE MARIA

Mother Mary is a figure *honored* primarily within the Catholic Church, and yet *ignored*, or even *reviled* by other religions or groups. **The Daughters of Heaven honor Mother Mary**—not in the traditional, religious sense, but rather as having a deep love and admiration, as well as a personal *connection* to Mary. They connect with her in ways that they, and others, sometimes can't even comprehend.

It often feels as though Mother Mary is a spiritual or angelic mother to the Daughters of Heaven—nurturing, guiding, and loving them. She was, and is, a perfect embodiment of the Divine Mother. That's why so many people around the world honor her by singing/chanting, "Ave Maria," which means "Hail Mary"—the salutation given to her by the Archangel Gabriel.

Mother Mary is the embodiment of the Divine Mother and the Divine Mother is the embodiment of Love. Therefore, Mother Mary is also the embodiment of Love.

HER CALLING CARD

The Daughters of Heaven can feel when Mary draws close to them by various "signs." **When Mother Mary is near, she often fills the room with the scent of roses**—the Western version of the Eastern lotus flower—that symbolizes spiritual awakening. Roses have literally been known to *materialize* out of thin air when Mary is present. Roses might also appear in a song, a photo, a movie, or an ad.

Those who are close to Mother Mary tend to favor the color blue, the color of Mary's robe. And what a person might assume is just a natural love of a particular color, is actually a subconscious awareness that this is the color associated with their Spiritual Mother.

This is *not* to say that a person cannot be a Daughter of Heaven if they do *not* feel a "connection" to Mother Mary. It simply means that it's a common occurrence to indeed feel an inexplicable connection to her.

MIRACLES, PROPHECIES & APPARITIONS

As the world currently continues to be transformed, **Mary is beginning to show up more and more—announcing firmly to all of God's Children (especially the Daughters of Heaven) that the time of the "Great Transformation" is upon us.**

Mother Mary has been manifesting to "visionaries" (almost always being children) for nearly two thousand years. Her most well-known appearances, however, were in Mexico—in the 1500's; Lourdes, France—in the 1800's; Fatima, Portugal—in the early 1900's; Garabandal, Spain—in the early 1960's; Zeitoun, Egypt—in the late 1960's; and Medjugorje (in former Yugoslavia)—in the late 1900's. These events are now known by the following names respectively: Our Lady of Guadalupe; Our Lady of Lourdes; Our Lady of Fátima; Our Lady of Garabandal; Our Lady of Zeitoun; and Our Lady of Medjugorje.

During these appearances, which have occurred on most continents and in dozens of countries,

Mother Mary is known to give messages, perform miracles, share prophecies, and show supernatural signs of her presence. What she shares with her visionaries include the following consistent messages:

1. The world, as we know it, will soon end.
2. Heaven shares a great sadness and concern for the condition of the world and its inhabitants.
3. The human race needs to have a change of heart and behavior, and make a commitment to change our lifestyles as soon as possible.
4. We should all pray for the world leaders and for those who are unkind to us.
5. The church has become corrupt and will pay the price.
6. There are ways to remain as safe as possible during the coming cataclysms.
7. All human beings need to come to a greater belief and faith in God and to practice daily prayer.

The people/children that Mother Mary has appeared to in these visions are, themselves, generally Daughters of Heaven. They lived lives as gentle, humble souls. Most of them were dedicated to their faith and to being prayerful, but some of them were just average people in most ways. All the visionaries agree that when they experience their visions of Mother Mary, they say she is beautiful— with a countenance that is supernatural. They also say she is very loving and gentle, even though there are times when she has shown them harsh images of the future on Earth. They describe her as the mother *of* all and the mother *to* all.

HAIL MARY PRAYER
(A New Version)

Hail Mary!
The embodiment of faith and grace.
The Spirit of Christ is with you.
Blessed are you among women,
and blessed is the fruit of your heart, Jesus.
Holy Mary, Mother Aspect of God,
pray for our souls to awaken,
now, and forever.
Amen.

CHAPTER EIGHT

The Daughters of Heaven & Mankind

MAKING A DIFFERENCE

There is no limit to the number of ways that the Universal Lightworkers—on Earth and beyond—can fulfill their soul's purpose. The same is true for the Daughters of Heaven. Both groups—which are really part of one group (the Children of God)—are making a positive difference in the world and in the lives of everyone they meet.

❧

God has given every soul a purpose. May we live that purpose. May we each lead the life that the Lord has assigned to us, and to which God has called us.

–1 Corinthians 7:17

As exaggerated as it might sound, **when a Daughter of Heaven enters a room, it's often as though the others in the room can sense that something** *holy* **has just occurred.** It's not so much the *entrance* of a Daughter of Heaven as it is the Spirit of God that they secretly brought *with* them. And one day, all the world will long to know this "secret" that these glorious souls are holding.

*If we love each other, God is alive in us,
and His love is brought to others in full
expression through us.*

–1 John 4:12

The Daughters of Heaven share their presence with the world, not so much by *preaching* it or *forcing* it upon others, but by *becoming* the change they seek to see in the world. **They are in love with the Divine, and they share this internal treasure with mankind through grace, a glowing countenance, the vibration of an inner knowing, and through their smile.**

They are usually gentle and not typically the type of person who would ever wish harm upon another. In fact, **they are usually known for being more forgiving and understanding than most people—**

even to the point of seeming to be "*too* loving" by some people. A great example of this endless reservoir of love is expressed well by Saint Teresa of Lisieux who once said, "Someday I want to go to hell because I want there to be at least one person in hell who loves God."

BEING OF SERVICE

The Daughters of Heaven are also commonly known to practice generosity and to be of service whenever they can. They are filled with generosity because they feel full enough that their cup overflows with goodness in so many forms that they feel inspired to share it. Their love for being of service makes it very natural for them to want to be around people and places where they can shine their Light.

***

Speaking to one another with psalms, hymns, and songs from the Spirit. Sing and make music from your heart to the Lord, always giving thanks to God the Father for everything, in the name of our Lord Jesus Christ.

–Ephesians 5:19-20

Like all other Lightworkers, **the Daughters of Heaven tend to gravitate towards hobbies, careers, and lifestyles where they can make a difference for mankind.** They tend to be mothers, healers, counselors, and so on. But whatever form of presence they choose, they are better at it than most because they care, they listen, they know, and they can see more clearly what needs to be done to bring "the greatest good for the most people" in any given situation.

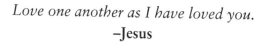

Love one another as I have loved you.
–Jesus

Their gift of love to mankind has barely been accessed by them, thus far, but will grow exponentially over the next several years as they learn to trust themselves. Sadly, although they feel tremendous love and devotion to God, they haven't yet completely accepted that same love for themselves. This is now changing, as **these blessed souls are being *activated* into the *remembrance* of *who* they are, their tremendous value, and *what* they are here to do.**

PRAYER FOR OTHERS
The I Am Song/Prayer

*(Jesus' words from the Acts of John—one
of the Lost Books of the Bible)
I am a light to those who see me. Amen.
I am a mirror to those who look at me.
Amen.
I am a door to those who knock at me.
Amen.
I am a way to those on the path. Amen.*

CHAPTER NINE

Archetypes & Role Models of the Daughters of Heaven

LEADING BY EXAMPLE

The clearest examples or archetypes for the Daughters of Heaven are similar to one another, and yet are also quite different. They are Mother Mary, Mary Magdalene, and a woman named Thecla—all of whom lived at the time of Jesus. Their *external* lives, personalities, and behaviors were quite different, just as such traits within any of the Daughters of Heaven might be different, but the *hearts* of these women were very similar: pure, courageous, devoted, and filled with grace—hence the statement, "Hail (Mother) Mary . . . full of grace." Despite their greatness as souls, there was absolutely *nothing* more important to them than being a "humble servant of the Lord."

The fact that **these women represent** *archetypes* means that *some* of their characteristics are likely to be found within most women (and men). Therefore, it would behoove the reader to consider which of these three archetypes most closely resembles themselves OR possibly consider how *each* of them is found within. In fact, we can also see the three maturing stages of a woman (from elder to woman to maiden) as Mother Mary (the elder), Mary Magdalene (the woman), and then Thecla (the maiden). Also, note that any *one* of these archetypes may resonate for one period of one's life, while another may resonate during another period.

Each of these archetypes overlaps a little in their definition, but they are also each distinctly unique in a few ways. The Magdalene archetype is unique from the other two women mentioned here in that this archetype embraces her sensuality a bit more. A Daughter of Heaven, therefore, can experience an affinity to Mary Magdalene and come across more sensual than she would if she were resonating with the matriarchal archetype of Mother Mary or the innocent maiden archetype of Thecla.

Being that **these three women are the most well-known archetypes (or role models) of/for the Daughters of Heaven,** it is essential that we share at least *some* amount of information about them, beginning with Mother Mary.

MOTHER MARY
(The conservative, mother type)

When Mother Mary was a child, she and her family were not traditional Jews per se. They were part of a spiritual community called the "Essenes." The Essenes were a spiritual, deeply devout community that lived in the region of the Dead Sea (near Jordan). They worked hard and prayed often—praying to God the Father and the Mother. They also recited daily prayers to specific angels every day.

Mary was one of a handful of female children who were "candidates" to become the embodiment of the Divine Mother, through whom the Christ Child would come. The Essenes prepared for this inevitable event for many generations. In fact, the name "Essenes" means, "Expectant Ones," and fits them very well, since they were the ones chosen by the Holy Spirit to prepare for the coming incarnation of the Christ.

This preparation of the Holy Mother took several generations of purification so that the blood, body, and mind would be suitable to carry such a special child in her womb. Also, Mary was put through numerous tests to confirm her strength and abilities to commit to all that would be asked of anyone with such a huge destiny. From the time she was a child, until the time she was sixteen she was subjected to long periods of prayer, fasting, meditation, and personal tests (or initiations). Eventually, one day, **during a spiritual festival, the voice of Archangel Gabriel was heard declaring that *Mary* was the one chosen to be the Christ Mother—hence the term "Blessed are you among women."**

After the crucifixion, resurrection, and ascension of her son (Jesus), Mary went—with her trusted group of supporters—to live out her final years in Glastonbury, England.

MARY MAGDALENE
(The free-spirited, but devotional type)

By now most of us have heard of Mary Magdalene. Unfortunately, the information about her life is so filled with past inaccuracies and present fantasies that we are left with an unclear portrait of her and her life. The stories vary from Mary being a converted prostitute to her being an Egyptian goddess. Strangely, the creators of these extreme variations have very little definitive proof of their theories, which are often founded on mistranslations and biased conclusions.

Some details about Mary have been "channeled," which tends to have some potential flaws due to the filtering from the channels themselves. This then results in drastic differences between the *channeled* material and the commonly accepted *historic* records. There are also several teachers and authors who tend to bully people into believing their version of Mary's life-story with the threat of ridicule to those who don't agree. These same individuals tend to exaggerate Mary's life, while simultaneously minimizing Jesus as being a mere mortal who was married, had children, and then died a natural death.

The Daughters of Heaven, however, have no interest in minimizing the role of the Christ Jesus, nor of the Divine Mother, nor of the three archetypal women included here. These women are clearly embodiments of the *real* divine feminine and are in need of no defense, nor do they need to have their roles exaggerated. Men and women who tend to be angry and controlling, or that allow fear to control their beliefs, are not likely to find themselves among the Daughters of Heaven.

Here are some of the essential and known facts about Mary Magdalene:

- She was physically beautiful and came from a wealthy family.
- She was the sister to Martha and Lazarus—the man who Jesus brought back from the grave.
- She experienced a major awakening after meeting Jesus.
- She tearfully and humbly came to him and washed his feet with tears and water, anointed them with oil, and then dried them with her hair.
- She was courageous enough to be at his crucifixion *and* his resurrection (when most of the others that were close to him fled for their lives).
- She became an important student/disciple of Jesus—before and after his crucifixion and ascension.
- In regard to the belief that Jesus and Mary were married, we can only say here that in Mary's own Gospel, there is no mention at all of such a thing.

Jesus is said to have cleansed Mary of "seven demons"—which indicates the cleansing of one's

flaws, limiting belief-systems, or character defects
that were trapped within her seven spiritual centers.
Once this cleansing was complete, she was able to
see the true nature of all things, and the transcendent
beauty of Jesus' teachings. In spiritual terms, **Jesus
opened and cleared her seven chakras** or energy
centers—making her an open channel to learn and
share the highest of his teachings.

⸎

*That which has held me in this prison
has been conquered, ignorance has died,
desire ended—the cycles of forgetfulness
are no more. Free at last, I will receive my
rest within the silence of eternity.*

–The Gospel of Mary Magdalene

When some of the Apostles asked Mary why the
Master was sharing such deep teaching with her (as
teaching a woman was against the standard custom
of the day)—teachings that had not even been
shared with the male apostles—she explained that
it was because they were *men*, and so they tended to
think they knew all they needed to know. She added
that she, on the other hand "completely believed

and trusted anything and everything her Master told her." This, she said, was why she was able to hear and learn so much. **She was completely open and teachable.**

After Jesus' ascension, **she left the Holy Land with the Holy Family (Mother Mary, the Apostle John, Joseph of Arimathea, Martha, Lazarus, and others), and ended up in the South of France** with her band of followers. There she lived for over thirty years in the seemingly endless honeycomb-like caves of the Pyrenees Mountains. These caves extend for hundreds of miles and make up the most extensive subterranean system in the world, making it nearly impossible to safely navigate the caves. Nevertheless, Mary was able to do so with her heightened level of clairvoyance (clear seeing)—that she achieved after having her third-eye opened and cleared by Jesus.

The "lost" *Gospel of Mary Magdalene* is unfortunately in very poor shape—missing large portions—thus it is in fragments. Nevertheless, **here are some of the most insightful comments from her Gospel**—which are things that Jesus taught her:

- "All things in the universe are connected with one another."
- "Man's belief in sin, and our actions that support sin, are what cause us to become sick and die."

- "Attachment to matter gives rise to passion against nature. Thus trouble arises in the whole body; this is why I tell you: 'Be in harmony . . .' If you are out of balance, take inspiration from your True Nature."

- "Matter is not bad, nor is anything that exists in the world—neither the *body* nor *sexuality* are *bad* or *sinful* of themselves—yet it is possible to make bad *use* of them, and we are all more or less sinners to the degree that we do not know how to adjust or harmonize ourselves with the Real."

- "All is pure to those who are pure."

THECLA
(The innocent victim, but courageous and tenacious type)

Thecla was a Pagan who was converted by the teachings of St. Paul. She was to be married but was so moved by Paul's teachings of Christ Consciousness—including the call to chastity— that when she refused to follow-through with the wedding, her fiancé and family asked the court to burn her at the stake for her disobedience. When the fires were lit, an unusual torrential rain came and extinguished the fire. She was released and went looking for Paul, asking him to baptize her, but he refused. His odd lack of interest and respect for her also led him to fail to make much of an attempt to assist her or support her when she was continually arrested, convicted, and sentenced to death.

Soon after, when she refused the advances of a local nobleman, he demanded that she be fed to the lions; but surprisingly, the *female* lion came and sat at her feet instead of attacking her. The same lioness protected Thecla from the attacks of several other wild beasts that were released to kill her. The nobleman was so enraged, he had her tied to four bulls so they could run in different directions to rip her body apart. The ropes, however, fell to pieces. Seeing these numerous miracles, the authorities released her.

Finally, Thecla was put into a pool of sharks to be eaten alive; however, a lightning strike hit the pool and killed the sharks. But again, Thecla was not harmed. It was at this moment that Thecla called on the Holy Spirit to baptize her while she was still in the water—a request that was granted. From that point on, she lived her life as an ascetic—living a life of prayer and solitude in the mountains of Syria. And, as unbelievable as it may seem, even there in the mountains living all alone, there were further incidents of men trying to rape and harm her. But, fortunately, time and again, Thecla was miraculously saved.

She lived in a cave in those mountains in constant prayer until she passed away at ninety. She was accepted as a Saint, and **because her faith converted so many people, the Catholic Church stated that she was "an equal to the Apostles."**

Thecla was eventually sainted and revered by many, but few people know of her mainly because she refused to conform to what the people and the culture demanded of her. Typical of a Daughter of Heaven, she didn't need the acceptance of others in order to fulfill her soul's purpose on Earth. Instead, **she created and accepted her *own* baptism and developed her *own* relationship with God.**

CHAPTER TEN

The Prayers of the Daughters of Heaven

WALKING IN THE LIGHT OF GOD

The Daughters of Heaven practice both *prayer* and *meditation* on a regular basis but to them, it's not work and it doesn't require effort. They thoroughly enjoy doing both—sometimes several times per day. They love to pray in *every* way: prayers from the heart, forgiveness prayers, affirmation prayers, the Lord's Prayer, prayers of praise, and prayers for the specific—or general well-being—of themselves or others.

Like most people on the spiritual path, the Daughters of Heaven take walks, exercise, and read books. The difference is that the Daughters of Heaven use moments such as these to enter into a prayerful or meditative state with God, Jesus, or the Divine Mother. In this state, they search *not* for lights, colors, nor any other of the various "special effects" that might occur in meditation. Instead, **they prefer to receive a sublime *feeling*—one of peace, love, and possibly reassurance that all is well and that they are indeed walking in the Love and Light of God.**

LIVING IN A STATE OF PRAYER

The Daughters of Heaven are much like the mystics of old. **They start and end each day with heart-felt prayer.** They also include prayer throughout their day—sometimes spontaneously and other times on an "as needed basis." Their style of prayer might be a traditional prayer (e.g. the Lord's Prayer) or it might very well be a prayer that reflects their feelings in the moment. Therefore, it might be a prayer of need, of thanks, of praise, or simply a prayer of personal conversation with Jesus or the Holy Spirit. **The most common theme behind the prayers or attitudes of the Daughters of Heaven is, "Here I am, Lord! What would you have me do!?"**

Pray without ceasing.

–1 Thessalonians 5:17

One of the greatest gifts we can give to mankind is the gift of our prayers. And the gift of our prayers is enhanced by our awareness that we are all ONE—all connected—spiritually and energetically. Therefore, the Daughters of Heaven only pray for others to receive what they, *themselves*, are willing to receive. Likewise, prayers for themselves reflect only that which they wish for *others*. The Daughters of Heaven have learned to pray less often with the word "I" and more often with the word "we."

In other words, the prayers of the Daughters of Heaven are not exclusively for *themselves* nor *others*; they are for us *all*. In the past, prayers for ourselves or others were typically based on someone having *external* issues and praying for those issues to *improve*. Now, however, Christ is teaching the Daughters of Heaven to "hold in their hearts" all that they would have once prayed for. Then, to imagine how it would feel if the desired outcome were *already* so.

Their prayers are not always an established set of words or sentences. They are more *personal*, like a heart-to-heart conversation with their Brother Jesus or their Divine Mother—the Holy Spirit. They love prayers of forgiveness and "decree" prayers. But **they pray more often to feel the *Peace of God* within themselves and others, rather than praying for the *material* or *mundane* things of life that have little or no *real* value.**

BODY & HAND MUDRAS
AND MANDALAS

Besides prayer itself, there are also invaluable gestures of the hands and body that support the practice of prayer. They carry deep symbolism related to opening ourselves up to God. These physical gestures are known as "body mandalas" and/or "hand mudras." The following are a few of the most common and most powerful:

1. **The Gesture of the Chalice**—This is done by having our hands held up to the heavens so that the body takes on the shape of the Holy Grail. This grail (cup/chalice) stands firm in the stem with its arms extended from a humble heart, waiting to be filled by the Holy Spirit or Divine

Mother. The reason Jesus is known synonymously with the Holy Grail is because he was filled with the Living Waters of the Holy Spirit. As we stand with our hands and arms (and heart) outstretched to the heavens, we can slowly and sincerely say something such as, "Here I am Lord. Use me as You *Will*, so that I may bring Your Presence to the world today."

2. **The Sign of the Cross**—This is a brief statement and hand mudra that is great at the start of any prayer, as it affirms that all we are about to pray for is being done in the Name of God. This is done by touching the tips of the fingers of one or both hands to a few specific parts of the body, (each step below symbolizing one part of the Divine Trinity), while simultaneously reciting the following statements: a) "In the name of the Father," as you touch your forehead— symbolizing God in Heaven (found in your head). b) "And of the Son," as you touch your heart—symbolizing the Christ who descended into the body and material world (found in our heart and torso) c) "And of the Holy Spirit," as you touch the two points of your shoulders, one at a time or simultaneously, symbolizing the Divine Mother who Guides us on our journey in

the material world (found below our shoulder-line).

3. **The Sun Salutation**—This is a well-known set of yoga postures that assist in stretching (opening) the body forward, backward, and side to side. It only takes a few minutes to complete, and can be repeated once or several times in a row. Adding the words of the Lord's Prayer to the Sun Salutation ritual is a great way to increase its level of power and effectiveness.

FORGIVENESS PRAYERS

The following prayer combines the Hawaiian Ho'oponopono prayer with the teachings of *A Course in Miracles*, and encompasses forgiveness and healing of the consciousness of all involved—both the giver and the receiver. Here, we are asking for our minds and perceptions to be healed, while affirming that it is already accomplished. The words of this prayer can be directed *to* ourselves or *to* others. It can also be said *for* ourselves or *for* others.

Ho'oponopono: "I'm sorry."
ACIM: I am sorry for forgetting your true identity and judging you as being capable of being sick (poor, depressed, etc.).

Ho'oponopono: "Please forgive me."

ACIM: Please forgive me for having projected my unhealed wounds and limiting beliefs onto you, thus co-creating your challenge. I also forgive myself, for I too have suffered by allowing you to bear the cross of my issues.

Ho'oponopono: "I love you."

ACIM: I love you because of who you truly are—God's perfect and Holy Child—the Christ.

Ho'oponopono: "Thank you."

ACIM: Thank you for mirroring to me that which needed to be Recognized, Accepted, Surrendered, and Refilled with the Presence of Truth (the Truth of who we are). As we now stand forgiven (by each other), we also stand healed and one in God, as God. And so it is!

Prayer is a way of asking for something. It is the medium of miracles. But the only meaningful prayer is [not for things but] for forgiveness, because those who have been forgiven have everything.

–A Course in Miracles

BLESSING OURSELVES OR OTHERS

When the Daughters of Heaven pray, like most people, they draw from a variety of options (e.g. prayers for healing, prosperity, the condition of the world, etc.). But they also have in their repertoire, one completely different kind of prayer—a type of prayer that was once reserved only for "great Saints" of the distant past. These prayers are known as "Blessings."

Blessings are different than most forms of prayer. Standard prayers often focus on the need for a solution to a problem, or they are sometimes based on feeling grateful for the miraculous solution that came about. Blessings, however, are *not* done or shared while we are in a state of *need*. Instead, the Daughters of Heaven have to imagine being in constant connection with God (which they are), and from *that* state of mind, they simply imagine the Love and Light of God filling them, and being poured out upon others.

The Daughters of Heaven offer their Blessings (of God's Love) to *anyone* and *everyone* who enters their mind *or* to whomever they see in a given day. These Blessings are like having an abundance of water and then walking into a group full of people who have been stranded in the desert. A person with a good heart and soul would naturally walk up to each one of those people and offer them a drink of water. There is very little time to discuss *why* they are thirsty nor *how* they ended up stranded in that desert. All that matters is that *they* are thirsty and *we* have water.

Similarly, when Blessings are given, they are shared unconditionally, as **there is no time nor interest in judging or evaluating *who* the recipient is nor *why* they might be in need.** In fact, we are *not* necessarily Blessing a person because they are in *need* (although we might do so). Instead, we are Blessing them *only* because they entered our mind or walked into our field of view. We certainly can share a Blessing to someone who is in need, but more often, Blessings are being done all the time— to *anyone* and *everyone*.

Although the Blessing comes *through* a Daughter of Heaven, the *Source* and *Power* of the Blessing is *God*—the Holy Spirit or Divine Mother. **The Holy Spirit knows very well *who* we are Blessing and the best way to *utilize* or *distribute* the Blessing.** In return for the many Blessings we bestow upon our brothers and sisters, each and every day, the Holy Spirit will also bestow special Blessings upon us.

EXAMPLES OF BLESSING PRAYERS
(Said out loud or in silence)

*Into your soul, dear brother/sister, I bestow this
Blessing, from God's Heart to yours.
In the name of Jesus Christ, the Holy Spirit of
God is now Blessing you with a wave of (Insert:
healing, abundance, etc.) and well-being.
And so it is!*

. . .

*In the name of Jesus Christ, I call upon the Holy
Spirit of God, to Bless you with the gifts of grace
and forgiveness.
And so it is!*

. . .

*Peace! Be still my brother/sister; I am Blessing you
with the I Am Presence of God!
Amen!*

. . .

*The peace that I Am, I Bless you with now!
Amen!*

CHAPTER ELEVEN

The Books of the Daughters of Heaven

BOOKS & TEACHINGS ARE NOT ALL CREATED EQUAL

The Daughters of Heaven are more easily defined by their *internal* state of being than by their *external* state. Nevertheless, we can learn a lot about these beings from their external practices—such as their choice of reading material.

Like most people on the religious or spiritual path, the Daughters of Heaven enjoy reading. However, they are finding themselves less and less able to settle for just any old spiritual, or self-help topics. They might enjoy some of these materials from time to time but they most enjoy, and insist on, the deepest, clearest materials. They are not looking for books or teachings that are too wordy nor too complicated. They know that **the Love and Truth of God are simple; therefore, reading materials related to God should also be clear and simple**—at least in most cases.

⌇⌇⌇

Simplicity is very difficult for twisted minds. Nothing is so alien to you as the simple truth, and nothing are you less inclined to listen to.

–A Course in Miracles

The Daughters of Heaven love reading books related to peace, nature spirits, healing, Jesus, devotion, angels, the Divine Mother, and materials that have a palpable presence of the Christ Light. **They read materials and watch inspirational video presentations that are uplifting, rather than depressing. If there is any sign of harshness, judgment, condemnation, or fear they usually stand up, turn around, and walk the other way.** Most importantly, they do so without judging those materials—knowing that such teachings serve *someone, somewhere.* But, they know in their hearts that such teachings are *not* for them.

EXAMPLES OF GREAT INSPIRATIONAL READING MATERIAL

- *A Course in Miracles*
- *Aquarian Gospel of Jesus the Christ*
- *God as Divine Mother*
- *God Calling*
- *Heart of A Course in Miracles*
- *Impersonal Life*
- *Jesus Calling*
- *Jesus the Son of Man* (Kahlil Gibran)
- *Mother Mary & the Undoing Process*
- *New Testament*
- *Paramahansa Yogananda* (Various titles)
- *White Eagle* (Various titles)

CHAPTER TWELVE

Conclusion & Summary

It would be unfortunate if this material was used to announce the *activation* of the Daughters of Heaven but failed to point out that the main point of their existence is to help facilitate the activation of the Christ Presence within ALL of God's Children. The Daughters of Heaven are here, answering God's Call to manifest "Heaven on Earth." They are now incarnating as "spiritual midwives," helping to birth the Christ within all of God's Children, and making the way clear for us all to return to Eden. These souls are doing their part by being of service to God the Father and God the Mother and God the Christ/Son (all of God's Children).

The Daughters of Heaven encourage all human beings to "live the Christ life"—surrendering all parts of our life and being to Christ Jesus and to the Holy Spirit (the Divine Mother). They also encourage all human beings to do their best to *behave* like the Christ by being loving, forgiving, compassionate, generous, and understanding.

❧

Brothers and sisters, rejoice! Strive for full restoration, encourage one another, be of one mind, live in peace. And the God of love and peace will be with you.

−2 Corinthians 13:11

As a reminder, this material is not just a book; it is a time-released "activation"—and the time for its release is now! Two thousand years ago, Mother Mary was pregnant with, and gave birth to, the Christ Child. Now, **we are *all* pregnant with this Holy Being—our inner Christ. Mother Mary and the Divine Mother are working with the Daughters of Heaven to bring this Child forth.** It's up to us to say yes!

AMEN!

Appendix I

AN INVITATION

It can be said that the Daughters of Heaven are a "*group* of *individuals*"—which means that they are partly a group and partly individuals. As individuals, they can act interdependently, following their own heart and soul as inspired by the Holy Spirit. As a group, **they are part of a greater collective, held together *not* by the traditional framework of a human organization, but by an energetic container resembling one ball of Light held in the Hands of the Divine Mother.**

Not being an official organization doesn't mean there should be a lack of a healthy and safe network that might prove helpful to the Daughters of Heaven—where they can gather to share their experiences—through *virtual* meetings and *actual* events.

We now invite those of you who truly feel a resonance with this material to join us on social media and our events. Here we can share ideas, experiences, and mutual support, as the consciousness of this group evolves. We do, however, insist on posts and behaviors that are based in love and authenticity.

You are welcome to join us in the many (often FREE) programs we offer to help activate the Daughters of Heaven and to assist the Earth *and* its inhabitants with our ascension process. This includes our virtual programs and groups on Youtube, Facebook, and Zoom. You can also join us for our in-person Sacred Sunday Services and occasional workshops hosted from The Global Center for Christ Consciousness in Sedona, Arizona. Lastly, you are welcome to join us in our full, 12-hour "Day of Prayer" (on-line) the first Sunday of each month.

PEACE BE WITH YOU ALL!

Appendix II

TESTIMONIALS FROM SOME OF THE DAUGHTERS OF HEAVEN

After the first announcement about the Daughters of Heaven (in a live talk), we received hundreds of letters, sharing the physical, emotional, energetic, and spiritual responses people had from listening to the talk on this topic. Many of these can be found on our website. The following testimonials are only the first couple dozen that arrived. These are not included here as promotional material or testimonials for this book, but rather, because of their ability to add to this teaching. Most of them began with the following: "When Michael said the words, 'the Daughters of Heaven . . .'" But we deleted these opening lines to save space here and to avoid being redundant. So please, just imagine those words at the start of each quote.

. . .

It was "the pause that was heard around the world," as Michael spoke (as always) directly from Holy Spirit's Guidance. He paused to clarify that yes, now was the time; that they are ready to be revealed. And in those few moments, time moved in slow motion for those of us in the room and watching live online. We could feel something big, something special, something new was coming. Filled with tender emotion the pause was audible. Then came the words, "Daughters of Heaven." The words flowed as eloquently and gently as the harmonies of a rainbow. The Daughters of Heaven are here; now; holding space; bringing God's Light back to our hearts; back to Eden; Heaven on Earth. We are grateful for this time of their reveal. To know of them, connect to them, and to be part of them. For now is the time! ~BP, FL

. . .

It struck me in a way I don't quite understand yet. This deep release happened . . . like a silent cry but with all the expressions and feelings of something being brought up from the pit of my being. ~NM, Ireland

Something overwhelmed me so completely that I gasped and then I wept—not emotional tears but tears from deep within me unlike anything I've ever experienced. I felt an unprecedented spiritual activation and integration. It was a release of something deep and treasured, a multitude of life experiences which fell into place like that of a mosaic. Shockingly brilliant synchronicities became epiphanies. This was a beautiful call to all Universal Lightworkers to anchor the presence of GOD.
~DBK, AL

. . .

I immediately felt a rush of warm energy flow through my body. My ears perked up as I hung onto every word. All of it rang true to me on a deep level. It feels like Daughters of Heaven is a name for something I've always felt . . . since childhood. It explains a lot of my life's experiences. ~JH, MD

. . .

This new theme—the Daughters of Heaven— woke something up deep inside of me. It was like saying, "Yes . . . I recognize myself." When I heard, "Daughters of Heaven," my heart said, "YES! This is me!" Thank you. ~MT, Finland

Wow, the very words—Daughters of Heaven— seem to carry light codes, and information beyond just the meaning of the words. I find that a lot of this material has evolved my understanding of consciousness and my place in the world.
~GS, Nicaragua

. . .

Shortly before you introduced this topic to the world, I was slightly saddened/confused as to why I had no discernable spiritual "gifts" like those of my friends. But during your talk, I experienced the MOST PROFOUND sense of peace. This peace came from the realization that all desire to "work" my way 'up the spiritual ladder' and achieve a "title" was gone. I no longer have desire to become more ascended, more anything. I'm ok to just love God. That's it! Pure and simple. I am at peace now with that. ~JF, Sedona

. . .

I felt a palpable hush, like time stood still. I knew to listen closely as something deeply beautiful and mystical was stirring the atmosphere and preparing to enter our awareness. Thank you for sharing these magical and important insights. ~LN, FL

I was awe-struck. The essence of those few words deeply resonated within my heart and soul and provided me with a profound understanding of my life experiences. ~MT, Canada

. . .

My mouth dropped to the floor. There are now so many unfolding synchronicities. For as long as I can remember, Mother Mary has shown up in my life in seemingly peculiar ways (as I've never identified as catholic). I have always related to both her and Jesus and have been graced with their love, healing, and teachings. The Divine Mother has been a pillar in my life and for that I am grateful. I know what Michael is sharing has so much to offer to so many people because this essence is like no other. To have Michael sharing this wisdom and beauty with the world helps me feel not only seen but expanded and dropped into the heart. ~DT, CO

. . .

I had recently been feeling drawn to the Divine Mother. From Michael's teachings a veil was lifted and I felt myself running to the Mother. Now I feel the Mother speaking to me and I feel as if She is holding my hand. She is now the real Mother I never had. I am a Daughter of Heaven. ~LP, TX

I began to feel an amazing radiating resonance in my body, mind and soul! I sensed this enthusiasm in my spirit like an angelic waterfall of love from my head down my back into my heels, and grounding me. I literally started to dance. It was immediate. I understood my life purpose. I'm forever grateful.
~LD, TN

. . .

One miracle in my life was coming back to God and Christ Consciousness through Michael Mirdad. Another was the message he shared about the Daughters of Heaven, which reconnected me on the deepest level with my Heart and Soul. Now I know and feel, I am definitely going home!
~NMS, Germany

. . .

The most amazing thing happened to me. I began to cry for no reason as your words hit home. Happy tears flowed, like a soul cleansing was taking place. My heart chakra blossomed and I felt at last I've found what my soul's been searching a lifetime for. I am honored to be part of the anchoring and spreading of Christ Consciousness and our Divine Mother's Love. ~JM, Scotland

I felt a blanket of peace and love envelope me. I had a sense of understanding why I'm here. I've never fit-in with any group—neither Christian nor "spiritual communities." After hearing of this topic, I have had extraordinary feelings in my solar plexus and heart chakras. I feel like I'm shining like a Christmas tree. It's an incredible feeling. I can't put my experience into too many words. I used to wonder why I was so different from everyone . . . sometimes screaming to the heavens . . . and now I know. ~TS, Australia

. . .

Something in my Soul was stirring as I listened to this topic. I will never forget the moment Michael paused and looked down and choked up for a moment. My heart was doing a cartwheel. I knew it was something profound. When he looked up and said, "The Daughters of Heaven," I burst into tears. Then the words, "It's been activated!" came to me. So I know that the energy of the Daughters of Heaven has been activated in the world. My world and my life now make sense. ~GD, Australia

. . .

Hearing of this was like finally finding my 'tribe' . . . like I actually "belong" somewhere." It just

helped me understand me, my life so far, my way of being, thinking, doing, saying . . . everything. It was as if Michael opened a door that I didn't know was there. ~KLF, Athens/Greece

. . .

I felt a feeling of higher vibration go through my being. My Right ear started buzzing and my heart filled with joy. I connected to the deeper meaning of my life experiences and what they were all about. ~BM, WY

. . .

My breath stood still. And in this silence, I felt a peace that can only be defined as Divine Grace. I wept tears of joy in that moment, and I felt the Presence of Divine Love. The strength of the message amplified, for we all felt it flow through us at the same time . . . a feeling of Hope. ~AM, Ontario, Canada

. . .

I had warm tears rolling down my cheeks, followed by compassionate feeling that just mushroomed up inside of me, prompted by vivid images of how much the Daughters of Heaven have kept their grace even in times of trouble and hurt. I am amazed by how much strength

they had in hardships, how much kindness and patience with this hellish world. It almost felt like a long-awaited recognition for their glow that they selflessly shared with others in need.
~JP, Serbia

. . .

There was a feeling of coming home and the ending of a long-lasting search for what this life is all about. Now, every time I speak the words "Daughters of Heaven," I feel such a deep gratitude and a natural connection to them. I am so filled with peace and appreciation for the Divine Mother pushing this information through the veil and out to humanity. Love and tears of joy—we are coming home!
~VES, Austria

. . .

I started to feel a small buzzing, like a gentle vibration in my whole being but mainly in my head/ crown chakra area, I even felt a bit light-headed. It was strong and beautiful. I loved what I was feeling. Then I felt very strongly the palms of my hands being activated, I saw a bright white light and a strong vibration, but at the same time felt so loving and gentle. It's like an activation started and it's not going away, I'm deeply grateful for this. ~JB, Mexico

Other Books by Grail Press

Healing the
Heart & Soul

Michael Mirdad
$18.00

The Heart of
*A Course In
Miracles*

Michael Mirdad
$20.00

You're Not Going
Crazy...You're Just
Waking Up!

Michael Mirdad
$18.00

An Introduction
to Tantra and
Sacred Sexuality

Michael Mirdad
$18.00

The Seven
Initiations on the
Spiritual Path

Michael Mirdad
$18.00

Creating
Fulfilling
Relationships

Michael Mirdad
$18.00

The Book of Love
and Forgiveness

Michael Mirdad
$18.00

Mother Mary
and the Undoing
Process

Robin Rose
$18.00

To order any of our books or request more information on any of
these publications, please call our office (360) 671-8349 or visit
www.MichaelMirdad.com for a complete list of books, CDs, and DVDs.

About the Author

Michael Mirdad is a world-renowned spiritual teacher, healer, and author. He has worked as an intuitive healer and counselor for over 40 years and is the author of the best-selling books *Healing the Heart & Soul*, *The Dark Night of the Soul*, *Creating Fulfilling Relationships*, *The Book of Love and Forgiveness*, *The Heart of A Course in Miracles*, and *You're Not Going Crazy...You're Just Waking Up!*

Michael has facilitated thousands of classes, lectures, and workshops throughout the world on Spiritual Mastery, Spirituality, Relationships, and Healing and is commonly referred to as a "teacher's teacher" and a "healer's healer." He has been featured as a keynote speaker in the world's largest expos and conferences and has been on radio, television, and various internet and tele-summit programs. His work has been published in several leading magazines, including *Sedona Journal*, *Conscious Life Journal*, *Spirit of Sedona Magazine*, and *Yoga Journal*, as well as being the cover feature several times in *Evolve* magazine.

Michael Mirdad is respected as one of the finest and most diverse healers of our time and is well-known for his ability to share the deepest spiritual teachings in a clear, applicable manner. For more information visit his website or Facebook page.

www.MichaelMirdad.com

www.facebook.com/michaelmirdadteacher